Map: The Wartime Adventures of B Squadron 'Corpse'

The 11th Battalion Royal Tank Regiment's 'Buffaloes' transport the assault forces to South Beveland and Walcheren, to free the Scheldt estuary and the port of Antwerp, a critical contribution to victory. Previously all supplies had to be moved by lorry from Normandy. As the Allies advanced into Europe, such long-distance supplying became uneconomical, the lorries using more fuel than they transported.

This map serves to conclude the largely frivolous early chapters on our 'Phoney War' and to usher in our 'Real War', which was very serious.

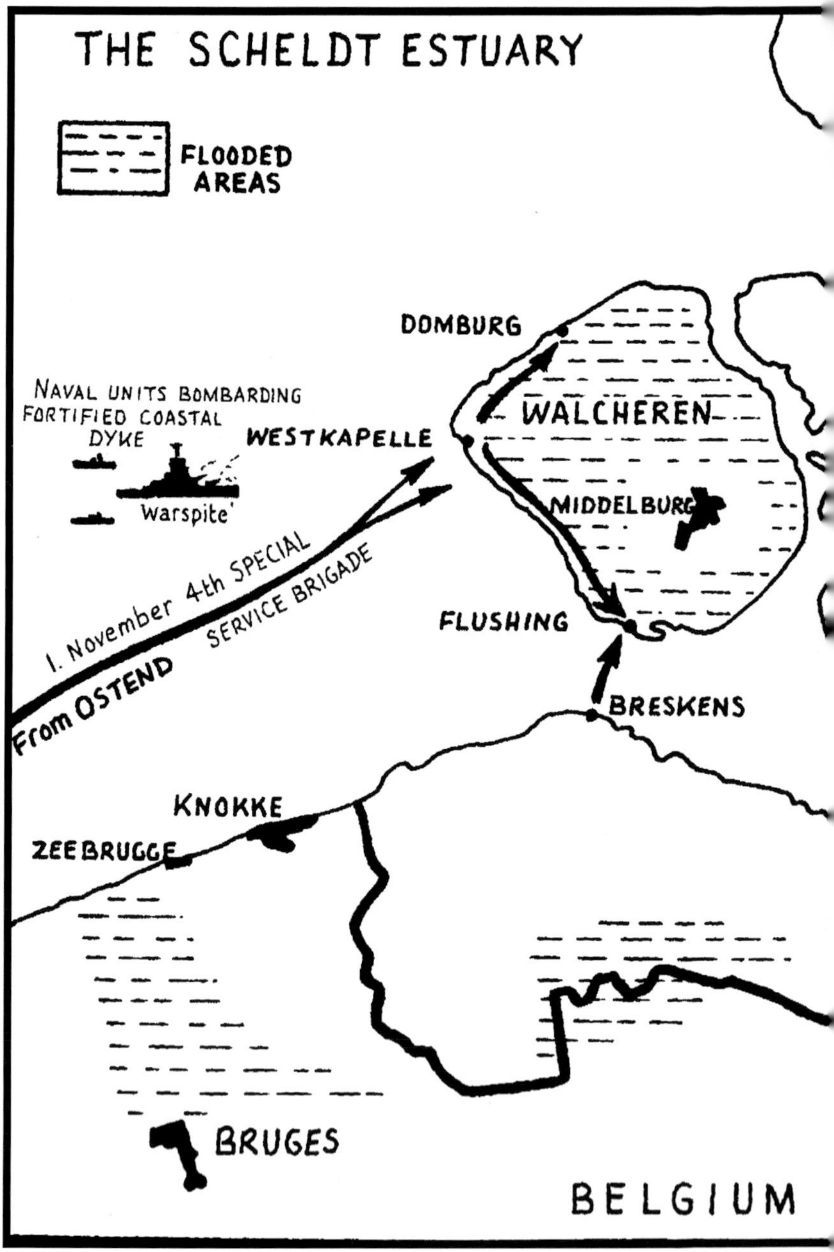
THE SCHELDT ESTUARY
FLOODED AREAS
DOMBURG
WALCHEREN
NAVAL UNITS BOMBARDING FORTIFIED COASTAL DYKE
WESTKAPELLE
Warspite'
MIDDELBURG
1. November 4th SPECIAL SERVICE BRIGADE
FLUSHING
From OSTEND
BRESKENS
KNOKKE
ZEEBRUGGE
BRUGES
BELGIUM

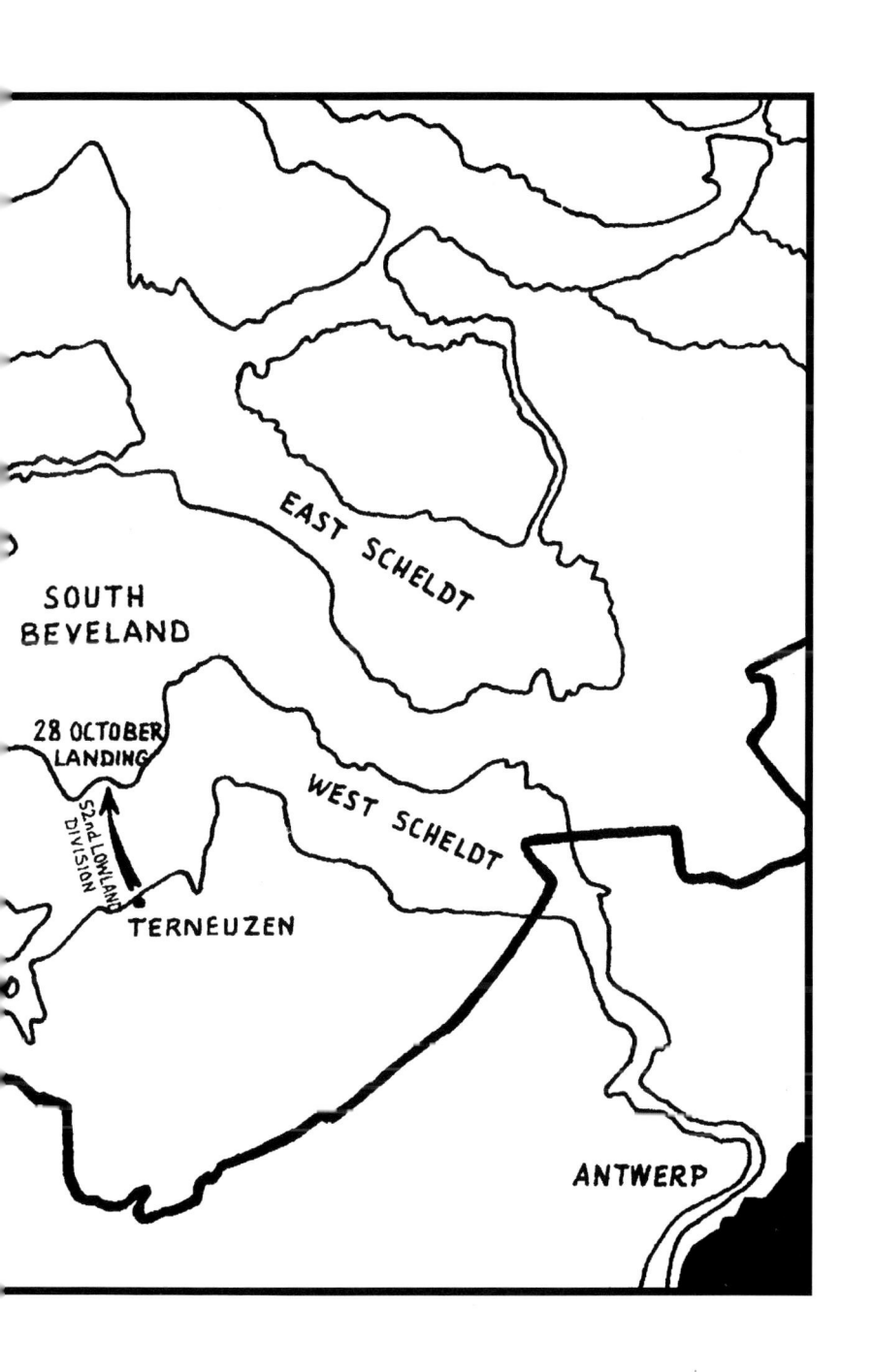

SOUTH BEVELAND

EAST SCHELDT

28 OCTOBER LANDING

52nd LOWLAND DIVISION

WEST SCHELDT

TERNEUZEN

ANTWERP

THE WARTIME ADVENTURES OF B SQUADRON 'CORPSE'

Maurice Wilson

PARAPRESS LTD
Tunbridge Wells · Kent

In the same INTO BATTLE series:

Across the Lines – An Account of Axis Intelligence and Sabotage in Italy 1943-1945
by Donald Gurrey OBE
Bombs and Barbed Wire – My War in the RAF and Stalag Luft III
by Geoffrey Willatt
Into the Blue – A New Zealander in the Royal Navy
by Captain T.D. Herrick DSC*
Let Go Aft – The Indiscretions of a Salthorse Commander
by Cmdr H.G. de Chair DSC*
Soldier On! by Brigadier Joe Starling CBE MC DL
Some Letters From Burma by Tom Grounds
They Gave Me a Seafire by Cmdr Mike Crosley DSC*
Triumph and Disaster – The Autobiography of a Naval Officer
by Cmdr Victor Clark DSC*
Wren's Eye View – The Adventures of a Visual Signaller
by Stephanie Batstone

© Maurice Wilson 1997
ISBN: 1-898594-30-9

First published in the UK by
PARAPRESS LTD
12 Dene Way
Speldhurst
Tunbridge Wells
Kent TN3 0NX

A catalogue record for this book is available from the British Library

All rights reserved. No part of this publication may be reproduced, stored in a retrieval system or transmitted in any form or by any means, electronic, mechanical, photocopying, recording or otherwise, without prior permission in writing from Parapress Ltd, Publishers.

Printed in Great Britain by
Biddles Ltd, Guildford and King's Lynn

Contents

Illustrations — iv

Preface — v

1 The great adventure begins – life of a recruit in January 1941 — 1

2 We prepare for one of the war's most bizarre activities — 16

3 Shorncliffe – we hinder the defence of southern England and I acquire my one and only war wound — 33

4 The 11th Battalion goes to sea — 45

5 The era of B Squadron 'Corpse' in the Holy Land — 50

6 Beyond the Holy Land — 68

7 Normandy, and Belgian interlude — 78

8 The Scheldt – our first brush with the enemy — 86

9 Walcheren – our Commando operation — 93

10 We hang out our washing on the Siegfried Line — 117

11 The Rhine – we storm the moat of the robber baron's castle — 120

12 Over the plain and far away — 134

Illustrations

Cover shows a Buffalo amphibious transport vehicle landing from the Scheldt with its usual almighty splash. The Buffalo was not a tank, just an unarmoured transport vehicle operating equally well in the water or on soft ground. Steering was by braking one track or the other. Its weapons were an Oerlikon 20 mm gun, firing cannon shells, and a Browning machine gun.

1. Matilda tanks in battle array.
2. A Matilda tank with standard 2-pounder gun.
3. Matilda tank with CDL turret.
4. C Squadron Buffaloes parked before loading troops of the 52nd Lowland Division for the attack on South Beveland.
5. Just after typhoons had attacked.
6. In the perilous 'gap' at Westkapelle, shortly after the first landing.
7. One of 79th Armoured Division's special vehicles, a 'Crab' adaptation of a Sherman tank, landing in the 'gap'.
8. Near Antwerp, October 1944. Monty inspects a V2.
9. Sir Winston Churchill speaking to men of 11 Royal Tanks; beside him Field Marshal Montgomery.
10. Churchill, mounted in a Sherman tank, smoking one of the cigars which became his trademark.
11. Churchill ceremonially crossing the Rhine.
12. The Prime Minister, accompanied by senior officers, making a ceremonial crossing of the Rhine in a Buffalo of B Squadron 11th RTR.

Cover picture, and pictures 1, 2, 3 and 10, are reproduced by kind permission of The Tank Museum, Bovington, Dorset.

Preface

Dear Reader,

I hope our unusual title may have caught your attention, but you may well wonder how a 'Corpse' can write a book. Here is a brief explanation.

B Squadron 'Corpse' was an 'alter-ego' I invented for myself as a means of countering the crashing boredom of B Squadron, 11th Battalion Royal Tank Regiment's sojourn in the, then, Palestine desert in 1942/43.

It arose partly from my being, at age 27, a sort of father figure in a unit consisting mainly of 20-year-olds; I was the 'old man' of the Squadron and, presumably, comparably incapable and inept. From this, arose the concept that I was virtually 'dead' though, amazingly, I am still sufficiently alive, at age 84, to write this book.

It has been said that warfare consists mainly of long periods of boredom punctuated by occasional intervals of fright. The boredom bit is certainly correct, but my own experience was a little different.

Though I took part during the latter part of the war in two very exciting battles, I cannot honestly say that I was ever particularly scared. Rather, I was just very interested in what was going on. Monumentally uncomfortable at times, yes, but stimulated rather than scared. I do not regret one moment of it.

I was also privileged to have some most interesting travel at the expense of HM Government, for which I am duly grateful and which I now share with you, my readers.

I have made fun out of the Army's wartime incompetence, but also acknowledge that the professional Army of today is something quite different. Most of those who took part during World War II were, after all, only amateur soldiers. Fortunately we had, on the whole, very competent, professional leadership and, in particular, the inspiration of the late and great Winston Churchill. He may have made the occasional mistake, like CDL, a description of which appears in this book, probably uniquely, but he was still one of the greatest war leaders of all time.

I am proud to have played a very minor part in Britain's 'Finest Hour'.

Maurice Wilson, 1997

1
The great adventure begins – life of a recruit in January 1941

One of a motley and generally scruffy collection of mostly very young men, I left the train at the nearest local station of my first Army 'home', the magnificent residence of the Duke of Portland, Welbeck Abbey. This was an example of the aristocracy making their contribution to the war effort by offering their homes as training establishments.

The first surprise was that the newly formed 11th Battalion Royal Regiment bothered to send an officer to greet this first draft of some fifty men, mostly from the woollen manufacturing area of West Yorkshire. The second, on arrival at Welbeck, was to discover that though we were quartered in one of England's prime stately homes, we were not to participate in its magnificence. In fact, we were shepherded into the former stables.

On the way, I was pleased to discover that there was at least one other educated man in our draft. Strangely, we two remained in close contact for the whole of the four and a half years of our war service and I was sad to lose contact with him on demobilisation. We both started with ideas of applying for a commission, but neither of us made it, both finishing as we started, as humble Troopers. Evidently neither of us possessed the necessary military mentality, or the mechanical aptitude to operate tanks. Later, I was to bring an important Army exercise to a halt through my mechanical incompetence, and my friend, Leslie Myers, was to be similarly responsible for my only war injury.

We two afforded an example of how two talented men could be totally wasted, to the nation's loss, by being used not only in the wrong job, but in the wrong field. Myers, a bright and handsome young man of 30, was sales manager of a Bradford woollen manufacturing company, and must have been, had there been no war, at the start of a successful career, for he also had social connections, being a friend of the then head of the Rowntree chocolate firm. Sadly, he was also one of very many men who lost the beautiful girl he was to marry during that early period at Welbeck Abbey. I only hope he was luckier in later life.

I was then 27 and fondly imagined that my experience in having started my own business at age 25 would have helped my Army career, but not a bit of it. Experience in managing men did not count, though later my main career was to depend considerably upon an ability to persuade others, of official rank far exceeding my own, into doing what I wanted.

Myers and I arrived at the stables first, thinking that thereby we should secure the best accommodation, but we miscalculated. Having the choice, we opted for the upper stable loft, with the later arrivals getting the ground floor, which we later discovered had two stoves to our one and was also less draughty, making a difference of about ten degrees in the temperature. Additionally, I got it wrong by choosing an upper berth in the two-tier bunks, draughtier than the lower. However, I was learning. When it came to filling our palliasses from an enormous pile of straw, I emerged with a full one, while latecomers were left with little to insulate them from the wire bases to the bunks.

Then came the next shock: our first meal. By January 1941, the civilian population was already suffering under food rationing, and it was surprising to find that the Army was generous, even wasteful, in the quantity of food offered to the troops. The dining hall was new, an enormous steel-framed structure, with long trestle tables running the length of the building sufficient to accommodate the, now, 300 men in our draft. At one end, a row of cooks ladled out about a quart of tea into our tin tea basins, and dollops, from a thing about the size of a hip-bath, of what turned out to be a mixture of cheese and potato. This hardly looked appetising, but turned out to taste excellent. We helped ourselves to two massive hunks of bread topped by about a civilian's week's ration of margarine. I found these last difficult to get down but, again learning quickly, found them easier to cope with if toasted in front of the stove.

We then found, to our dismay, that we had to clean our own plates, etc., and that there were no washing up facilities whatsoever. We had to swill them off as best we could, under the one tap, cold of course, in our stable barrack room.

I happened to be detailed for 'fatigues' on this first day so, with two or three others, had the horrific job of cleaning up the disgusting mess left on the tables after the meal. This was a real shock. During my earlier career in landscape gardening I had become used to living in working-class lodgings, and thought I should know what to expect. But the usually kind, considerate and houseproud landladies belonged to the now almost vanished race of the respectable working class and bore no resemblance to the men, mostly from poor families, who made up the bulk of our draft. I just could not believe that human beings could voluntarily make such a mess. The Army laid great emphasis on good order, and always insisted on everything being clean, for inspection. But it never seemed to occur to the Army authorities how much easier it would have been if they had prohibited the making of a mess in the first place. The same thing happened with the barrack rooms. In those days, practically all young men smoked, and most of the litter on the floors consisted of cigarette ends. Every morning, the barrack rooms were inspected, and a massive clean-up operation was known to be necessary in preparation – but it never seemed to occur to anyone that all this effort could have been saved by precautionary measures.

Here, we had an example of an unfortunate human trait: people en masse always behaving in a way they would never do individually. Though most of these young men came from poor homes, most of these would no doubt have been well regulated within the limits of the family's means, with a mother in charge who had to be able to manage scarce resources if all were to survive. This mother, also, particularly if she had a large family, would have had to maintain reasonable good order for the household to function. So, if her spoilt adolescent son made a mess, she would clean it up for him, and it never occurred to him that this was not part of the natural order of things, and that he might one day not have a female slave to wait on him. For British working class society in the 1930s was still male-dominated to a degree that would be quite unacceptable in the 1990s, whereas boys from middle-class homes, particularly if they had been subjected to the rigours of a public school, were not waited upon by their mothers and, perhaps surprisingly, had a much harder life than their working-class contemporaries.

In my own case, I was somewhat older in actual years, but vastly older in experience than these 20-year-olds. Far from being waited upon, I had had to be fairly self-sufficient from the age of ten, having, during my mission school in China period, suffered far worse conditions than the Army in wartime had to endure. Further, even when I returned home for school holidays, my Mother was already developing rheumatoid arthritis and it was a case of me looking after her, rather than the other way round. So, during these early days at Welbeck Abbey, I suppose I must have been something in the nature of a mother-substitute, with the Army hierarchy acting as substitute father.

After the shock of the dining hall it was pleasant to discover that the Army also had its own form of civilisation, in the shape of the YMCA supplied and fitted up by that imaginative granddame, our patroness, the Duchess of Portland, a contemporary and, I later discovered, a personal friend of that ultimate embodiment of English aristocracy, the late Queen Mary.

This establishment offered such facilities as a radio, piano, writing tables, easy chairs, darts, table tennis and a food counter where one could buy what small luxuries were available at the time. Not surprisingly the YMCA was immensely popular, for it provided more comfort than most of the men would have experienced at home.

An imaginative touch was provided by an officer who had been a pre-war political agent, who organised a concert to welcome the recruits. Anyone who could provide any kind of a turn was invited on to the stage, and it soon became apparent that the new battalion was not lacking in talent. Most offerings were, of course, contemporary 'pop' songs but there was also one young man who, but for the war, might have had a significant career in the entertainment industry. He brought the house down with a glorious rendering of the tenor song 'So Deep is the Night'. Another case of a talent wasted by the war.

From the Elysian heights of the YMCA, it was down to earth with a vengeance, to washing as best we could at the barrack room's single cold tap before 'lights out' at 10.15 pm. Early in 1941 one of the earliest utilities to disappear was razor blades, and I remember with horror, having to teach myself to manage a cut throat razor at this cold tap.

And so, in the words of the immortal Pepys, to bed, and, the stove by now having gone out, to a cold, draughty and vastly uncomfortable night.

The next morning, after breakfast consisting of porridge (one dollop), sausages (three large) and the usual hunks of bread and marge, the rabble spread out all over the stable yard, now the parade ground. The kind and fatherly drill sergeant, whom I remember with some affection, reduced them to some sort of order in remarkably short time. His technique was gentle persuasion combined with reminders of the terrible things that would happen to us if the dreaded sergeant-major were to take over from him. The latter, a loud-mouthed, dark-jowled natural bully of an Irishman, was indeed someone to be avoided. Not for nothing have so many of history's tyrants been former NCOs, notably our adversary, Hitler.

One event was the issue of uniforms, clearly so much more suitable for the occasion than our ill-assorted civilian clothes. Also the recruits, not being yet properly dressed, were not allowed out of camp until they were. Most men, noting that at least it had no brass buttons to clean, as the excellent quality greatcoats had, were pleased with their battledress. Having a well-developed chest, I found my battledress fitted well though most of the lads needed the squadron tailor's alterations.

At this early stage, the Army introduced us to what has always been one of its strongest policies: developing pride in the unit and inculcating a belief, usually false, that there was something special about it. However, the Royal Tank Regiment did have a difference. One was designated 'Trooper' not 'Private' and belonged to a squadron not a company. One carried a ·38 Smith and Wesson revolver, not a rifle, as personal weapon and one sported the distinctive black beret, which, worn well, gave a distinctly racy appearance. In fact, the unit retained something of a 'cavalry' atmosphere. Though, when we were issued with our 'Matilda' tanks they were classified as 'infantry tanks', tanks generally took over the far ranging functions once performed by the cavalry.

On the third morning, our drill was taken over by a magnificent-looking lance-corporal, one of the few former regular soldiers drafted into our new battalion. Most of these few were obviously drop-outs, with a very few survivors of the former 2nd Battalion RTR which had been badly mauled by General Lord Gort's one, failed, counter-offensive in the 1940 Battle of France. Had Lord Gort had at his disposal even three times as many Matilda tanks as he had in fact, he might well have succeeded and turned the tide of the unstoppable German Panzers, thus possibly altering the whole course of the war. One of history's many might-have-beens. I later learned that the first 2 pounder gun we used for instruction purposes came out of the Imperial War Museum – such was the scarcity of all weapons at this stage.

Our lance-corporal, with splendid cavalry moustache and a beret worn at a rakish angle and pulled well down to the right ear, looked rather like Kitchener must have looked as a young man and gave the impression of being the ultimate professional soldier. I suspect a lot of this was just for show, but he said he had seen actual hostilities on the Indian North West Frontier. In our subsequent experience, my squadron suffered precisely *two* men killed during its entire existence from January 1941 to Autumn 1945. What a contrast to the casualty rate of the First World War. I often wondered since what subsequently happened to the flamboyant Lance-Corporal Henshaw. He also is remembered with affection.

One broad Yorkshire fellow volunteered for clerking in the Squadron Commander's office. A resplendent officer – it might even have been the Colonel in person – entered and asked for some foolscap paper, to meet with the bland reply 'Ee, 'ave only joost coom, ah don't know where now't is around 'ere.' This was capped by another, particularly scruffy Yorkshire type, who continued wearing his woollen vest until it began to stink and was asked by his mates why he did not change it for the second one with which he had been issued, to which he replied 'Ee, 'ave I got anoother one?' Evidently it was unknown in his home in the 1930s for anyone to have a second one of *anything*.

Drill on the fourth day was not made easier by a liberal covering of snow, accompanied by a biting wind. However, again, my experience made it easier for me than for my fellows for I had been in the OTC at school and already knew all about drill, equipment, etc. Initially this led to my being selected as 'marker' for the parade to form up upon. However, I was soon replaced as skill developed generally, by someone taller and, no doubt, more soldier-like. I never managed to look remotely like a soldier, even after four and a half years.

Much enjoyed by all was our first shower, which unfortunately revealed two men with lice, in the very nicely fitted-up shower shed donated by the Duchess. Much ribald laughter was caused when someone spotted Her Grace, always interested in everything that was going on, peering through her lorgnette through the window at the boys showering.

Another occasion was our first contact with Welbeck's magnificence, in the shape of our first PT class in the underground ballroom, with the sprung dance floor serving splendidly to aid our exercises, while from the walls the portraits of numerous ancestors of the ducal family looked down, probably disapprovingly, upon our clumsy efforts where elegant ladies in crinolines once disported. The ballroom was said to have housed 1,000 people in comfort.

That evening I made my first faux pas. In going for a walk in the park, with a few others, we ducked heads to avoid the driving snow and, in the process, missed seeing an officer. We were summoned back in stentorian tones by our corporal, mentioned before, who wanted to know what we meant by failing to salute an officer, as instructed, stating that he would probably get his (appendages) chewed off by reason of our negligence. We returned in a spirit of proper contrition at having let our corporal down. I, at least, should have been less distressed at having let down our squad officer in charge of the barrack room, an Irish ex NCO who had evidently, in preparation for his commission, gone to the trouble of taking elocution lessons and acquired the artificial 'cut glass' accent fashionable for the upper classes in the 1930s. He was promoted to captain before we left Welbeck and probably had a successful Army career, but I never took to him.

Our training was clearly rushed through as quickly as possible, as our Matilda tanks would be urgently needed for the Middle East campaign. It was a little like going back to school, with the day divided into hour-long periods, which left our 20-year-olds sadly disillusioned with soldiering, and many of them homesick. Their poor physical condition was illustrated by several faintings during the drill sessions. There was even one suicide. I felt positively paternal towards some of these lads, and at 27 positively old and experienced. I came to the conclusion that the wartime Army was all right for a man, but precious hard on a boy straight from home.

A second glance of the glories of Welbeck Abbey came from attending a church service in the highly ornate private chapel. The old Duke, in person, read the lesson, with the Duchess sitting just behind me. Significantly, only a few of the troops attended but *all* the officers.

After three of our five weeks' training we began to move with the easy precision of the Guards in Whitehall and the sergeant major began to regard us with conscious pride, instead of describing us as 'pregnant ducks'. We began to snarl and bare our teeth at each other if anyone made a slip on parade, in our anxiety to preserve our proud reputation. What little things please people when their life is reduced to such triviality! Eventually, there was universal joy when the snow at last disappeared, to give firm ground underfoot.

As training progressed so did the piles of equipment with tin hats (never actually used during our active service), anti-gas capes, also never used for their intended purpose but more effective as a waterproof than the ground-sheet capes provided for that task, water bottles, mess tins, overalls, etc., in fact just about everything except that very basic requirement, handkerchiefs. I was kept going when I had a cold solely by being sent old sheets from home. Most of this had to be exhibited at morning barrack room inspections, built into neat little pyramids to specified design and crowned by tin plates and mug – which always fell off. Our pretty patterns were praised on the special occasion when inspected by that semi-divine personage, the Colonel, gratifying for me because I had missed breakfast that morning putting other men's blankets into correct order. Our squad officer was less easily pleased, however, and enquired 'Who the hell we thought we were, the French Army, perhaps?' This was a particularly cruel joke at that time, coming so soon after the French collapse in 1940.

After five weeks we at last got down to the basics of weapon training. I was amazed at the destructive power of the, even then, outdated ·303 rifle but unimpressed with the weapon itself, particularly after one of them blew up in the hands of our gunnery officer as a result of a bent barrel, leaving it looking like an inverted umbrella.

Of course, it was impractical to use a rifle in a tank, and everyone was pleased that we would be having revolvers – kept in thigh holsters – on account of the difficulty getting through the tank's relatively small turret hatch. Revolver training, however, was disappointing, particularly to anyone familiar with Wild West films in which victims are picked off by revolver fire, on galloping horses. Not only I, but no one in the group with me, proved to be able to hit a static man-sized target at a range of ten yards. It was perhaps as well that our battalion went right through the four and a half years of our active service without anyone ever having to fire a shot. Still, that ·38 Smith and Wesson became almost part of oneself, and I was indeed sorry in October 1945 to hand it in, together with the original twelve rounds of ammunition, completely unused.

Though again we never had an opportunity to use it, the weapon that impressed me most was the very accurate Bren gun, the Czech-designed light machine gun which was at least as good as its German equivalent. Not until the 17 pounder appeared relatively late in the war did we have a tank gun anywhere near as good as the famed German 88 millimetre; quite the best weapon produced by either side during the war. The 2 pounder gun with which our Matildas were equipped had the very high muzzle velocity of 1,750 feet per second, but the 2 pound projectile was too light to damage heavy tank armour. The Matilda, with 3-inch-thick turret armour, was reckoned to be relatively safe, as tanks go, but all the tank men I met who had seen combat would rather have been in the infantry, where one could at least get to ground even if not dug in.

Last of all the weapons to reach us was the basic one, our tanks, but at last they began to arrive in quantity from the tank manufacturers, Fowlers of Leeds. I have an idea that the workers at Fowlers must have been going through a bad period when they produced my metallic home which was to stay with me for some three years. The consumer fondly imagines that all products which are mass produced ought to be of comparable quality, but sadly it is not so. The British have always been imaginative in giving romantic names to their weapons of war, and so it was with our battalion's tanks. Those in B squadron were given the names of impressive birds, the names of the three tanks in a troop beginning with the same letter. Ours were Kestrel, Kittiwake and Kite.

Somehow, it seemed natural justice that the worst tank in the entire battalion should be named Kite, the despised scavenger bird of the Middle East. In practice, Kestrel and Kittiwake proved to be average tanks, though neither of them was ever as good as, say, Heron, one of those in our accompanying two troops. Throughout its undistinguished life, Kite was always holding up the highly co-ordinated movements which later became essential to our function because it could never be persuaded to a speed of more than 8 mph. This, despite the constant and dedicated efforts of the squadron's fitters. To this day, I do not understand this, for the squadron's other, apparently identical tanks, on average, produced a speed of about 15 mph. Perhaps I, as probably the least mechanically minded man in the entire British Army, exercised some kind of jinx over it. Anyway, it also seemed natural justice that our worst tank and least competent crew man should be associated.

As the full complement of tanks arrived, so rumours of imminent action, probably in the Middle East, proliferated. But suddenly counter rumours that instead we were to go for further specialised training at Penrith in Cumbria began to replace these. It was the latter which turned out to be correct, for our time at Welbeck Abbey was to be followed by a full year in the environs of another stately home, Lowther Castle, near Penrith, the seat of the Earl of Lonsdale, whose predecessor introduced boxing's Lonsdale Belt.

This seems to be the time to reflect upon a period which proved to be, in my estimation, a significant turning point in the life of this nation. For I believe the Second World War, rightly said to have produced Britain's finest hour, a time when everyone worked, unselfishly, to bring about the downfall of one of the worst tyrannies the human race has ever seen, also sowed the seeds of the present declining nation of the 1990s.

Our time at Welbeck Abbey was one of intense activity, but too much of this seemed at the time, and seems to be still, to have been futile, irrelevant and grossly wasteful of time and resources when we were supposed to be preparing for total war.

Take the example of food. At a time when the importing of food was costing the loss of thousands of seamen's lives, and the decimation of Britain's once great merchant shipping fleet from German U-Boat activity, our small unit, at the time numbering some 400 men, was consuming huge quantities. We used margarine at the rate of half an ounce per man per meal, with 50 large loaves. Some 15 complete legs of mutton were cooked for a main meal: about 1,000 sausages for breakfast. A day yielded a dustbin full of scraps for pigswill – nearly as much as was eaten. This I know for a fact, having all too frequently been on the fatigues having to clear up and collect the mess.

But worse was the waste just of manpower. The Army, judging no doubt rightly that idleness would lead to loss of discipline, was always desperately anxious to keep everyone fully occupied. But the snag was that the Army had almost no real work to do, so had to manufacture artificial tasks.

This ran absolutely contrary to the experience of men like myself who were used to working very hard for long hours. Even the twenty-year-olds who had not had time to accumulate much personal work experience, knew that hard physical work dominated the whole lives of their parents and families. They knew what it was like to work in the coal mines, the iron and steel works, or even as navvies. It used to be a matter of pride to young men at that time as to how *fast* they could work, and their elders, who after a lifetime of toil could no longer work so fast, were often despised.

Suddenly, at this most impressionable age, the nation's young men were faced with, instead of doing what in their world was considered a man's work, such tasks as polishing brass buttons, darning their own socks, endlessly cleaning up the barrack room, kitchen fatigues, etc. The kind of thing they were used to seeing their mothers do – women's work. Not unreasonably, even the least intelligent of them invariably resented this. So, there developed the Army technique of 'scrounging' or avoiding as far as possible all the tasks the Army set them to do. This might not have mattered as applied to the tiny number of men who constituted the peace-time Regular Army, but it did very much matter when it applied to a fair sample of the whole population.

These young men, when the war ended, had to go back to civilian employment and real work again. But by this time, after four or five years of 'scrounging', they had, like the long-term unemployed of the 1990s, lost the habit of real work. Some, indeed, I heard myself at the time announce openly that they never intended to do any work ever again, and too many of them kept to this resolution, no doubt encouraged by the union-dominated period following the war. Certain it is, that the landslide vote which, to many people's surprise, put a Labour Government in power in 1945 came considerably from disillusioned ex-servicemen. They were not really voting for a Labour Government, but simply against authority in all its forms, and against the compulsory system of futile time wasting to which they had been condemned for the whole war period.

Nor was our unit in any way untypical, though from the nature of the specialised role we had, we probably wasted more time than most. The Second World War involved minimal casualties when compared to the horrific slaughter of 1914-18, or even of the American Civil War, one of the reasons being the generally more adequate standard of leadership, with a deliberate policy of avoiding casualties. It was this last which made Field Marshal Montgomery so popular with his troops – though his officers generally hated him. The troops knew very well that he was not going to risk their lives unless there was absolutely no option.

Also, everyone who followed closely the history of the British Army in 1939-45, would know that the war was fought mainly by the same units, with casualties replaced as they occurred, but always leaving an experienced and battle-hardened core; not by replacing those units with others. Nearly every advance was spearheaded by the 7th or 11th Armoured Divisions. Other units were spared casualties simply because they were not employed in active hostilities. So, basically, most of those nominally 'on active service' actually had little to do.

Our last days at Welbeck Abbey, as it was now June and, at last, quite warm, passed pleasantly enough. Many men were now due for leave, but this meant even more 'fatigues' for those left behind and an account of what I actually did during a sample week, when allegedly undergoing 'intensive training' may interest today's efficiency experts.

Monday. Sports Ground fatigue. All I did was empty the motor mower grass box for the groundsman, sunbathing in the intervals.
Tuesday. Shifting kit bags in the Quartermaster's Stores, followed by potato peeling at the Officers' Mess. Whatever else was neglected, the Officers' Mess had always to be stuffed with men doing virtually nothing. Half of B Squadron not on leave were acting as batmen.
Wednesday. A day spent fiddling with our new tank, 'Kite'. Something useful I did learn in this connection is that if a piece of machinery is working satisfactorily, for God's sake leave it alone! When it goes wrong is the time to start fiddling with it. Being constantly instructed to grease its numerous nipples resulted in positive damage, in the form of breaking all the oil seals involved. At this stage I became thankful that I had qualified as a wireless operator (that is a general dogsbody), not as a driver-mechanic who was normally responsible for keeping the tank 'on the road'. Though, probably due to the previously mentioned 'off' day by the workforce at Fowler's of Leeds, I doubt whether any mechanical genius could have kept 'Kite' on the road.
Thursday. The same as Wednesday. We now found, or rather the fitters found, that in addition to faulty batteries and badly synchronised engines, one of the bogey-wheel cradles had broken and the wretched thing would probably be out of action for weeks. Had Hitler known about 'Kite' and chosen that moment to invade, he would probably have succeeded.
Friday. Stacking blankets at the QM Stores. The original issue had at last been replaced, to everyone's relief. Followed in the afternoon by assisting in the matter of the broken bogey-cradle.
Saturday. That most dreaded of fatigues – cookhouse, consisting mainly of trying to wash up massive greasy pans in cold water.

Sunday was not recorded, but probably consisted mainly of Church Parade as usual.

One or two very pleasant episodes preceded our leaving Welbeck Abbey; for example, a boxing display, headed by professionals, with prizes presented by Lady Anne Cavendish-Bentinck, a junior member of the ducal family. I had previously tried my own hand at boxing, but soon decided this was not for me in view of my 'hosepipe' of a nose. Needless to say, I did not wish to smear the beautiful ballroom with my blood.

Another very pleasant episode at this time was camping out in the park, by now, in June, in beautiful summer weather. In particular, I enjoyed a three-day stay at the neighbouring camp at Thoresby Manor, a spot even more sylvan and delightful than Welbeck. We were quartered in huts under the shade of a magnificent beech wood interspersed with horse chestnut. There were greens of all hues, from dark pine, fir and cedar, shading to the deep greens of beech and chestnut, the browny green of new oak leaves, the slaty shade of willow or silver birch, to the bright grass green of young larch. For contrast there was the gold of yew and cypress and the deep blood red of copper beech, with magnificent specimens of great size, yet almost as symmetrical as if they had been clipped. Added to this were the huge banks of rhododendron in full flower, the paler reds of hawthorn and the remains of some later fruit blossoms, the whole reflected in the placid waters of the lake at sunset. Truly, being in training in the Army of 1941 had its compensations. One wonders how much of this sylvan magnificence has survived into the 1990s. The English country house is surely one of this country's major contributions to civilisation; created certainly only for the few, but today available to the many at very modest charges.

Though much of our training at Welbeck was plain idiotic, and incredibly wasteful of time and manpower at a period when we were supposed to be preparing for total war against ruthless opponents, I cannot leave the ducal seat without praising some aspect of our individual training.

Being fair, those responsible for the training could not know how entirely unusual our occupation during most of the war was to be. As a wireless operator, which was my normal job, endless time was spent trying to master the Morse Code, though we never, in fact, had any occasion to use this during the whole four and a half years the war lasted for us. We used the No.19 wireless set a great deal, for our movements were co-ordinated through this, but always through open speech, not by Morse Code. Getting the whole battalion 'on net' or on the correct wavelength was always a preliminary to all exercises. Nevertheless, I spent far more time, particularly in view of the recalcitrance of our tank 'Kite', in helping to keep the poor old ruin going, than ever I did in operating the wireless set. In the last stages of the war, when 'Kite' had finally been ditched and we transferred to 'Buffalo' amphibious craft, we were no longer bothered by wireless communication at all. Then my main function became just raising and lowering the 'ramp' of the Buffalo, as she was loaded and unloaded.

So it was most inappropriate that, included in our initial training, was not only the Morse Code but also electrical theory. All the instructors in such specialised subjects were superb. Indeed, during a long, active career I have been privileged to listen to many high grade lecturers, but I have never heard another so brilliant as the corporal who attempted to impart to us wartime soldiers the intricacies of electrical theory. I only hope that after he passed from our ken some better use was made of his outstanding talent.

In general, Army education was superb. I would say that it was the thing the Army did best back in 1941. In most other things they struggled on as best they could in the circumstances.

The end of our initial training at Welbeck seems an appropriate moment to compare conditions then with those in the modern regular Army of the 1990s. Indeed, there is absolutely no comparison. As in everyday life, it is a different world.

The writer was fortunate, taking advantage of his previous wartime military background, to visit a regular army unit, the temporary depot at Brawdy, near Haverfordwest in Pembrokeshire, of the Royal Welch Fusiliers, now one of only three Welsh regiments to emerge from cuts and amalgamations in recent years.

This aged 'old soldier' was received quite splendidly, being met at the entrance to the camp by a resplendent corporal, equipped with stick of office, as camp guide. The first discovery was that eating is now handled by the NAAFI, in World War II the only provider of comforts and luxuries, thereby removing, at a stroke, the most unpleasant aspects of wartime Army life.

The dining room, preparing for lunch when I saw it, in pristine, gleaming perfection, was fully up to the standards of a superior hotel and the kitchen, all in stainless steel, looked to me as well equipped as the luxury cruiser on which I travelled on a Nile cruise last year. What a contrast to the glorified pigsty of dining conditions we suffered at Welbeck in 1941!

The next surprise was no more barrack rooms, as we knew them. The latest accommodation is of small but comfortably furnished individual rooms with personal television set: in fact, almost hotel standard accommodation. All this is for private soldiers, not those of high rank. This, to me, removes the worst aspect of Army life: the total lack of privacy we suffered in wartime.

Indeed, in the 1990s the Army's situation is precisely reversed from what it was in 1941. Then the problem was a surplus of manpower, and how to keep it occupied. Today men, even private soldiers, are a scarce and valuable commodity, carefully selected, and paid, I thought, very favourably up to the earnings standards of skilled men – which indeed they are.

Evidently, pride in the unit is as strong as ever today; I duly noted that most of the men in the Welsh regiments are still Welshmen, and recognisably so, and that the great traditions are preserved of, say, the South Wales Borderers, who won at the battle of Rorke's Drift, so admirably recorded in the film *Zulu*, the greatest number of Victoria Crosses ever awarded for a single engagement.

It was also interesting to see the obviously changed status of officers. The young captain who received me was clad in a working-type jersey, with no indication of his rank other than his, not very obvious, shoulder pips. He was busy preparing for a move, on to active service, for the unit. His corporal of the guard had the more elaborate uniform.

2
We prepare for one of the war's most bizarre activities

So in July we departed to our second stately home, or rather to its Park, for at Lowther Castle, Penrith, we never even entered into the castle itself except to attend classes there. Lowther was, in any case, not truly a castle at all, but rather a comparatively recent 'folly'. When I went back there, long after the war, it was to find that the structure had in the meantime been completely destroyed by fire, leaving only one entire wall still standing.

I recall Winston Churchill proudly announcing at the time when the very wet winter of 1941 arrived, that all troops in the UK were then under permanent cover. Sadly, it was not true, for when we heard this over the radio, we were only too conscious that we still lived in tents in Lowther Park and spent much of our time stepping between duck boards in trying to keep out of the all-penetrating, squelching mud. Unlike the hippopotamus of the Flanders and Swann immortal song, I found then, as I still do today, that mud is far from glorious. Our squadron contained a person whose hobby was the weather, and he reckoned that during the time we spent at Lowther it rained on 313 days.

But here it is appropriate to divert in order to describe how it came about that we were sent to Lowther Castle. And the matter was so complicated that, for once, the Army had to abandon its usual policy of telling those involved nothing about what they would be doing. We had to take an official oath of secrecy not to say anything about it for the duration of the war – and, amazingly, to the best of my knowledge no one ever did. No one I have spoken to since has ever heard about our unique wartime activity.

The great Winston Churchill was a highly imaginative man with a weakness for gadgetry and, of course, one has to remember the apparently hopeless position of Britain early in 1941 at the blackest time of the war, with the Nazi-Soviet pact still operating and the German U-Boat campaign sinking our shipping at a rate calculated to defeat us, certainly. Who could blame him for adopting any suggestion that held out a ray of hope?

Britain at this time was swamped with refugees from conquered Europe and many of them were among the leading intellectuals of their day. Such a one was the Czech optical scientist who approached Churchill at his most vulnerable and managed to sell him his pet idea. This device consisted of an ingenious system of attack by light, calculated to disable the opposition through dazzle and so prevent them firing back. I think he got the idea from ancient Rome, when the legionaries won a battle by burnishing their shields and using the sun's reflection to dazzle their opponents.

It worked in the following manner. On arrival at Lowther Castle, we removed the gun turrets from our battalion's tanks and replaced them with special turrets shipped from the United States where, evidently, their army command shared in the secret. In these turrets was mounted a carbon arc lamp generating 23 million candle power, of a brilliance that defied the human eye to look at it. This lamp reflected backwards on to a mirror on the rear wall of the turret and, from this, out through a narrow slot at the front, creating a 'wall' of light. The battalion's 60 tanks were then drawn up in line abreast at precise distances apart, so that the beams of light intersected, thus creating even greater intensity and ensuring that there was no break in the wall of light.

But the inventor's ingenuity did not end at this point: he added an armoured vane, oscillating in the manner of a windscreen wiper, which opened and closed the slot emitting the light, so that it created a 'flicker' so timed as exactly to defeat the human blinking mechanism. These oscillations of the armoured vane also had the secondary function of keeping out at least most of the machine gun bullets

Wall of light

which it was assumed would be fired at the lights in order to try to extinguish them.

It follows, of course, that for this system to succeed it had to be conducted with meticulous precision, for at no time must the wall of light be broken by removing it for an instant from the enemy objective. When the attack was launched it had to be presumed that it would be over rough ground, causing the tank to 'buck' as it passed over bumps or hollows. This in turn would cause an individual tank's light either to float up into the sky or to disappear into the ground, thus breaking the wall of light and making the system ineffective. But again, our ingenious inventor had anticipated this, though for this he had no mechanical answer: he had to depend on an individual soldier operator who could be subject to human error.

It was at this point that the man originally intended to be the tank's wireless operator, in this case myself, came into the picture. What he was asked to display was very considerable manual dexterity and lightning-sharp reactions, for he had to operate a hand wheel which controlled the elevation of the beam of light. According to the bumps in the ground the tank encountered, he had to rotate this hand wheel in one direction or the other in order to keep his beam on an even keel and, always, firmly fixed on the enemy objective. And all the other operators in the battalion had to be able to do the same, without fail.

In retrospect, I still marvel at the degree of drill precision which, over our long period of training lasting most of the duration of the war, was duly achieved. I suppose this must be accounted a triumph for the drill system, whereby it became so familiar one could have done it almost in one's sleep.

This, then, was the activity for which we had been moved to Lowther Castle, clearly selected as a remote and sparsely populated area where our activities would attract as little attention as possible, though I imagine that the inhabitants of Penrith, themselves restricted by the 'blackout' applying all over Britain after dark in those days, must have wondered about the flashing lights in the sky above the Lakeland Fells, which they could hardly have failed to notice. Anyway, if they did notice, the civilians, like our own personnel, kept the secret. Surely one of the most remarkable aspects of the whole war was the way in which vital secrets were kept, like the timing and site of the D-Day invasion in 1944, and the incredible way in which the German command were fooled into believing, even after it had taken place, that this was only a feint and that the real invasion was still to come in the Pas de Calais area. It was the success of this deception, backed by what was surely the finest piece of camouflage in the whole of military history, the American General Patton's 'phantom' army, supposedly assembled in East Anglia ready to invade, that won the war in the West for the Allies. If the German reserves assembled to repel this expected invasion of the Pas de Calais coast had been transferred quickly enough to meet the real Normandy invasion, the whole D-Day enterprise might well have failed. Then, the German Command would have been free to transfer the bulk of their forces in the West to the Russian Front and possibly Nazi Germany might conceivably have won the war. Another of history's many 'might have beens'.

We must have been very fully occupied at this time, for my war diary for the period is sparse. Our weapon, clearly, could be used only after dark, so the period at Lowther was spent solidly on night operations conducted on the barren and isolated Askham Fell, above Lake Ullswater, where our tanks were parked. Night after night we conducted, first, troop exercises, then ones on squadron scale and finally that masterpiece of co-ordination: a complete battalion tryout of the system. We paraded regularly at 7.30 pm, travelled by lorry up to the tank park on the crest of Askham Fell and worked all night, on occasion finishing as late at 5.30 am. After a particularly late night we were sometimes allowed to sleep till 10.00 am the next morning, but this was no substitute for a normal night's sleep and men began to crack up. Indeed, the Colonel was overheard to observe that he doubted whether the men could stand the intensity of training for much longer. In addition to the training, there was also the very serious job of guarding our secret weapon, which called for guard duty at terrifyingly frequent intervals.

About the only relief, which came more frequently to me than to most other men of the squadron, was when 'Kite' broke down as usual and spent another period in the hands of the squadron fitters, spread in pieces all over the Fell. They never, as far as I recall, managed to produce any real improvement. As observed before, constantly taking any piece of complicated machinery to pieces rarely helps.

Summer of 1941 produced some foul weather in August, but compensated with a beautiful September and October, giving an opportunity for the occasional outing to an enthusiast for the beautiful Lakeland country. I recall visiting the district's largest town, Keswick, twice. It seemed, then, the last surviving link with pre-war England, full of wealthy evacuees from dangerous areas. There were still shops containing filigree goldwork and Royal Worcester china; in fact it was still a town that did not know there was a war on. Even the local landscape painters seemed to be enjoying a boom.

Accompanied on most occasions by Lance Corporal Hill, the first NCO to be appointed from among our draft, I did some climbing in Patterdale, on Helvellyn and around Lake Ullswater. Hill was one of the few well educated and intelligent men in our squadron, and I then regarded his promotion as a hopeful sign, unfortunately rarely repeated. He was another with whom I was sorry to lose contact subsequently. On occasion we fell in with an RAF mechanic and his wife, people sufficiently well off before the war to own a yacht, who took us round in their car, cars before the war being the perquisite of the relatively rich. This man, too, was serving in the ranks.

Another pleasant change was volunteering to spend four days on the back-breaking task of potato picking at a local farm, but the work, to me, afforded a welcome break in the routine of night operations. This included two magnificent meals, with the farm's regular workers, in the huge farmhouse kitchen. I can remember to this day, the vast quantities of meat and potato stew doled out to us. The good food gave a real boost to my sleep-deprived state of health. I believe we were also paid a few shillings, old money, which must have been highly profitable for the farmer, for he had a lot of work done for almost no cost.

Indeed, good food was perhaps what I remember most vividly at Lowther – other than predominantly foul weather, and this was at a time when the bulk of the civilian population were really feeling the pinch of rationing. Well into 1942 hardly anyone seemed to eat in camp. My own favourite haunt was a certain pub, way up in Askham Village, just below the Fell, where the discriminating could still obtain a lavish meal of ham and eggs which helped to fortify one against the strain of night operations.

Most of the lads used to walk regularly the two or three miles into Penrith town partly in order to eat something other than Army rations, but even more to sample what all declared was the best beer they had ever tasted. The large town of Carlisle was farther away, about 20 miles, but I never heard of anyone bothering to go there, as Carlisle beer was despised compared with the much prized local brew. The Penrith pubs in the evening reverberated with the sound of jolly carousing. My friend, Myers, was among those who appreciated Penrith beer, for he, unlike myself, was a habitual drinker and used to maintain, I believe rightly, that his regular beer ration was essential to his good health. Certainly when the supply later dried up, he seemed to shrink. Two intelligent NCOs, Corporals Green and Goodman, used to declare that their hobby was beer, and they meant Penrith beer.

Myers and I, accustomed before the war to frequent hotels rather than back street pubs, would occasionally invade Penrith's George Hotel, much to the irritation of the battalion's officers, who regarded the hotel as their own domain. However, there was nothing in regulations to prohibit this, so they had to endure the presence of a couple of mere troopers enjoying their pre-war lifestyle. Last time I visited Penrith, only a few years ago, I was gratified to find the George Hotel still in business: a symbol of continuity in a fast changing world.

But these were just the interludes. The realities of life at Lowther were centred around our weapon, CDL*. On first arrival, we had to go back to school, attending lectures in the Castle itself by the learned scientific inventor, and on completion we had to take an exam in the theory of attack by light, so we had no excuse for not knowing our subject.

As the wretched winter developed, with longer and longer nights in which to practise, we churned the mud of Askham Fell even deeper as more and more of its once fair surface was ploughed by our tank tracks. At this point it may be of interest to note that I went back to Askham Fell 30 years after the war and there was then no doubt at all as to where our tank park was sited. Our tank tracks were still clearly marked in the sparse grass. It took a second visit, half a century after the event, for them to have disappeared entirely, when I found the wood by which we used to park was no longer there. Anyway I was then no longer sure where it was.

Those interested in preventing desecration of our landscape may like to note just how long it takes for really severe damage to the environment to heal. And this, bear in mind, was tough moorland grass, surely one of the most resistant of all plants.

* Canal Defence Lights. This name was invented to bamboozle the enemy.

In that Winter of 1941 the elements, as well as the German war machine, seemed to be against us. The rain seemed continuous, and capes (anti-gas) the only tolerably efficient waterproof we had, were put to much better use than that for which they had been intended; for that dreadful weapon of the First World War, the gas attack, proved to be yet another outdated way of waging war.

On nights when we were not actually practising, and ever improving our technique of handling the CDL light, some of us would usually be on guard duty, accompanied by our faithful Bren gun, though whether the latter would have been of much use in the never-ending, drenching rain I lack the expertise to say. On those lonely nights, with the silhouettes of our tanks looming out of the mist, I used to console myself with thoughts that some 2,000 years ago, Roman sentries must also have been on guard duty on such lonely spots as this: indeed we were not so far away from the terminus of the Roman wall at Carlisle. No doubt they were far from home, for Rome had its techniques for preventing subversion by sending its legionaries recruited, say, in sunny Syria or Egypt to man Hadrian's Wall, while the Britons would have been sent perhaps to the Transylvanian mountains in Dacia. The way the military mind works has not changed any more than has mankind's endless appetite for war.

It is surprising how it is the trivial incident that lingers in one's memory, while the great events tend to be forgotten. For instance, I have the clearest recollection of one particular guard duty on Askham Fell. The guard commander happened to be a newly recruited lance corporal, obviously a very decent and conscientious man of about my own age, or older. As one having mature views and conversation, I was immediately drawn to this man, particularly as he went out of his way to make the unpleasant guard duty as agreeable as possible by trying to conjure up a cosy atmosphere. Decent though he was, our lance corporal was also very obviously no more a natural soldier than I was. It so happened that someone with a particularly regimental attitude inspected the guard that evening and found fault with just about everything, particularly the condition of the Bren gun, which had been left permanently out in the rain and for which this particular guard commander could not reasonably be held responsible. I am not sure that our kindly guard commander was not placed on a charge. Perhaps it was the injustice of this that fixed the incident in my memory. Lance Corporal Janney also retains a soft spot in my recollections.

Finally our night operations culminated in a grand try-out of the CDL system towards the end of the good weather period, before the then General (later, of course, Field Marshal) Sir Alan Brooke, GOC Home Command. He, it was said, would give the final decision as to whether the scheme would be adopted, or not.

All members of the 11th Royal Tank Regiment had absolutely no confidence in it and hoped the great man would throw it out. For a time, it appeared he had done, for, from this time onwards, the intensity of night operations gradually dwindled.

I have an idea that this humble author actually owes his still being alive today to Sir Alan Brooke. One cannot, of course, do more than guess at this, but this most intelligent of wartime commanders later became Chief of the Imperial General Staff and, as such, one of the most powerful influences in Britain's conduct of the war. Without any positive evidence to this effect, I have the impression that he acted as a curb on Churchill's more extreme exuberances, of which CDL was an example. Every time, and it was only too often, the British Army became bogged down in the course of hostilities, Churchill wanted to use CDL to make a breakthrough. Rumours spread through the unit that we were about to take it into action, but every time someone evidently had second thoughts, for our secret weapon never saw the light of day, or rather the darkness of night, right up to the last stages of the war, and then not in our hands. What must surely have happened is that the General Staff at the last moment must always have overruled Churchill's wish to try out his brilliant baby's effectiveness.

Strangely, I do not remember much about the key exercise which represented the culmination of our arduous training at Lowther Castle. I seem to recall that it went well, with no significant breakdowns, and that the guinea pig infantry unit, acting as the enemy, and of course kept totally in ignorance of what to expect, were indeed completely surprised when our tank attack burst among them.

Nevertheless, I have the feeling that Sir Alan Brooke probably came to the same conclusion as I had myself, that the German command would not be so easily taken in. Though they would undoubtedly have been able to see nothing against the dazzle effects of our lights, they were not deaf and would have surely concluded, from the vast noise made by 60 close-packed tanks advancing in line on a broad front, that they were being subjected to some kind of a tank attack. Accordingly, they must surely have quickly concluded that firing machine guns to try to put the lights out was producing no result, and would instead have started firing their very effective anti-tank guns. Maybe their devastating 88mms originally designed as anti-aircraft guns, but later used so effectively as anti-tank weapons, would not have been available so early in the war as this, but they would surely have been able to knock out several of our line of tanks, thus breaking the wall of light and making our weapon ineffective. For certain, a good puff of wind would have been enough to dispose of our untrusty steed 'Kite' and with it your author.

So, the period of intense activity petered out and, with the advent of winter in late October, our camp in Lowther Park began to take on a more permanent appearance. More and more of our time came to be devoted to improving the camp, or just to more and more guard duties, while opportunities for outings declined. In due course sectional huts, long promised, began to arrive. By way of a typical British compromise, the greater number of tents – ours not among them – were re-erected inside marquees for protection against the frosts until such time as the huts were ready.

At this stage, a brief essay on the subject of 'mud' may be in order. First, there was the brown mud round B Squadron huts; pretty well churned up, but otherwise not too virulent and, at least, odourless. Next, the red mud round the NAAFI; somewhat deeper, this, sticky and difficult to remove. Then we had the black slime round the cookhouse, permeated with countless tea slops and vegetable leavings: rich in odour which could be smelt a quarter of a mile away. Last, we had the deep, well-churned creamy mud of the tank park, anything up to two feet deep, according to position; sour and green in colour and in places churned into a liquid mess which oozed in over the tops of gumboots – and stank to high heaven. No wonder the last took half a century to disappear completely.

The Royal Tank Regiment's motto was 'Through Mud and Through Blood to the Green Fields Beyond'. At Lowther we were well and truly introduced to mud. Later, although not in tanks but in Buffalo amphibious craft, we were fortunately spared much blood and I suppose the 'Green Fields Beyond' bit represented our triumphant progress across the North German plain by tank transporter in 1945.

As the night operations tailed off, these were gradually replaced by a reversion to general training. I obtained a driving and maintenance refresher course during which I was properly taught for the first time how to drive a Matilda tank on the road. I found that, even with a good tank, you could do only 18 mph at most. However, owing to the tank track's poor roadholding qualities, even this speed was quite interesting on a twisty road.

The Matilda weighed only 25 tons, so must have been easier to control than the much heavier tanks of the later war years, but keeping the vehicle on an even course solely by braking one track or another, instead of the simplicity of a steering wheel, called for a degree of driving skill.

There was also the opportunity to regain a little physical condition through some pick and shovel work. There was one, to me, highly enjoyable task in which B Squadron was called in to clear the main road over Shap Fell of snow. However, the improvement in physical condition was not enough to enable me to cope with being roped into the Squadron's cross-country running team and strangely, in the light today of still being around at over 80, I came to regard myself as being an old man at 27. Anyway, when I came in last, or 60th, from the latest run, the authorities were finally persuaded that cross-country running was not for me. It must have been around this time that I acquired the sobriquet of 'B Squadron Corpse', which name stuck with me for the rest of my Army career.

In due course Christmas 1941 arrived, not too unpleasantly, crowned by Leslie Myers, Jack Harris, another kindred spirit, and myself, upsetting the battalion's officers by having lunch and dinner at the George Hotel, Penrith. At this time, one could still get excellent food if one could pay for it.

At Penrith, as in Scotland, however, more was made of the New Year than of Christmas, with most of the local population, and all of the 11th Battalion, spending New Year's Eve dancing round the clock in the town square. So we had another, self-imposed, sleepless night.

After this, everyone was, needless to say, spent up and I had to plead with my family to send me a small sum to tide over until I had recovered from the position of total capital consisting of one shilling and seven pence (old money), borrowed. In return, I had to say in the words of a contemporary song 'I can't give you anything but love, baby. Love's the only thing I've plenty of, baby.' Amazingly though, the miserable Army pay of those days, for a non-drinker like myself, was generally adequate and I managed some very adequate 'leaves' subsequently with little or no financial restriction, proof, surely, that inflation is an even worse enemy that was Nazism.

Not the least valuable of our Christmas presents was that, at last, we were installed in Nissen huts instead of our tented camp. Of course, one can never have everything, for condensation forming on the walls would drop in dreadful 'plops' on those unfortunate enough to occupy top bunks. Those poor citizens who were incarcerated in Nissen hut air raid shelters during the air raids of this period will understand about condensation. As our huts contained a full troop of 18 men, we generated plenty of it.

However, the bunks were comfortable enough, and I cannot describe the joy of actually being able to walk upright again after living in a permanent crouch position. Also, with most of the canvas taken down it was possible to move about the camp without falling over guy ropes. The only real trouble was the continued lack of illumination, with three hurricane lamps per hut giving poorer light than we had under canvas. At this time the Penrith shops were overwhelmed with demands for candles, and cases of eye trouble, surely due to the permanent gloom in which we lived, landed our Medical Officer, trained as a vet, in something he was hardly equipped to handle. At least in the huts we were warm as long as the fire was kept in.

Perhaps the most unusual Christmas was that spent by one Lance Corporal Leffler, a South African soldier of fortune, who became official 7 Troop wit and was certainly a great character, whom I also remember with affection.

This man served in the Spanish Civil War and Abyssinian War of the 1930s and had been thrown out of pubs from India to San Francisco. He went to an OCTU (officer's training unit) on joining up, but was thrown out for drunkenness. A really nice and intelligent fellow, however, when sober, and a most entertaining story teller. On Christmas Eve he got himself 'blotto' as usual, and was picked out of the gutter by the local police. So, Jimmy Leffler was thrown into 'jug' for Christmas. On coming out he was loud in praise of the police and the grand time he had spent. He commented bitterly on how awful it was to come back to the Army after the comfort and courtesy of Penrith gaol.

And so, we duly came round to the momentous year of 1942 when allied fortunes in the war reached their lowest ebb, with shipping losses from the U-Boat offensive reaching their maximum, the Red Army reeling from Hitler's early triumphant blows in Russia, and the United States as yet not fully engaged in the war.

The Western Allies at this time were under constant pressure, understandably, from the Russians to start a second front to ease the intolerable pressure they were under, pressure which the western leaders were reluctant to refuse in case their wartime ally were to collapse, thereby probably ensuring that Hitler won the war. But, against this, they knew only too well that at this stage they simply had not the resources for anything like a Second Front, and particularly lacked the shipping and specialised landing apparatus necessary for making a landing on the heavily defended European coast.

So this was the year of the birth of Combined Operations, in which all the best military brains in Britain combined to produce the high degree of Army, Navy and Air Force co-operation which bore fruit in the brilliant, and decisive, D-Day landings, in June of 1944. But this was not produced without considerable pain and loss in 1942, culminating in the disastrous Dieppe raid in August of that year.

This operation, in which only the Commando operations against peripheral coastal gun batteries were successful, resulted in one of the most horrific Allied casualty rates of the war. Of 6,086 personnel engaged, 3,663 became casualties, including nearly 1,000 Canadians killed and nearly 2,000 prisoners, among them one brigadier and four battalion commanders.

On the basis of these figures, the Dieppe raid can only be classified as a disaster, for which the planners, in retrospect, cannot be wholly exonerated, to the extent even of allowing their battle plan to fall into the hands of the enemy. This author also cannot see why, granted that a battleship's support could not be risked at this stage, at least a monitor, providing one large gun, could not have been employed.

Against this, the RAF's air cover achieved a considerable victory over the Luftwaffe, causing the latter to call in reserves from all over France, Belgium and Holland and destroying some 96 enemy aircraft. But, importantly, the planners did learn from their mistakes, and they could learn only by trying out their theories in practice.

Among the important conclusions reached was that an assault on a strongly fortified port could not succeed; it had to be over open beaches. There had to be an overwhelming preliminary air and naval bombardment. There had to be much better specialised landing equipment. There had to be surprise by a force of sufficient strength, backed by sufficient reserves. All these requirements were later met on D-Day, including providing an artificial port, in the shape of Mulberry Harbour, ensuring quick reinforcement of the initial landing.

Of the essential requirements for success of our amphibious landing, the one that particularly concerns this narrative is the one calling for specialised equipment. The first step towards this was the establishment of the 79th Armoured Division, which having been formed as a normal Armoured Division in October 1942, was in April 1943 reconstituted as a Special Division consisting of tank and engineer units under the command of a single senior officer, Major General P.C.S. Hobart. It was said in our 11th Battalion RTR at the time, that General Hobart was directly responsible to Churchill, and not through the normal Army chain of command, which may explain why our CDL tanks remained in danger of being used until as late in the war as the Autumn of 1944.

This Division eventually became the largest all-armoured formation in the British Army and towards the end of the war was also its largest division. All the varied units were developed under great secrecy as our own had been. The assault Brigade of 79th Armoured Division was established during the Summer of 1943 as a result of lessons learned at Dieppe. This brigade included assault sappers carried in tanks and trained in mechanical placing of anti-concrete charges, operation of mine-clearing devices, assault methods of crossing walls and ditches, etc.

Their main vehicles were the 'DD' tank, an amphibious tank, developed from the American Sherman with a canvas 'skirt', making it waterproof enough to navigate at sea; the 'Crab', a Sherman tank with a rotating drum mounted in front of it to which was attached chains which beat the ground in front, thus exploding any mines in the tank's path; and the AVRE (Armoured Vehicle Royal Engineers), in British Churchill tanks with various attachments.

Most importantly, the AVRE operated the 'Fascine', a bundle of chestnut paling for dropping in a ditch, or on the far side of any steep drop to provide a soft landing for the tank; the 'Bridge' for crossing a wider ditch; the 'Petard', a short range missile discharger, particularly useful for driving right up to the slit in a concrete pill box and discharging its missile through the slit with devastating effect; the 'Bobbin' or carpet-laying device for making a firmer surface for following tanks, used for crossing stretches of soft sand, etc; and the Armoured Bulldozer. There was also the 'Crocodile' flame-thrower, mounted on a British Churchill tank.

All these devices played a leading part, subsequently, in the success of the D-Day landings, notably in reversing the procedure of landing infantry first which had caused such high casualties at Dieppe. Such of the coastal guns as had not been silenced by the preliminary naval and air bombardment were generally taken on successfully by the 79th Armoured Division's special tanks which also spearheaded the subsequent breakthrough into open country in France and the capture of the Channel ports.

Indeed, the only unit of 79th Armoured Division which remained unused was the CDL tanks, namely ourselves, which brings us back to 11th Battalion RTR still struggling in the mud of Askham Fell near Penrith.

During the first couple of months of the momentous year of 1942 rumours, rife at any time, proliferated fast. At a time when Rommel was rampaging in North Africa, the Japanese had conquered nearly the whole of East Asia and it was by no means impossible that the two might join up in India, while the collapse of the Red Army in Russia seemed imminent – they had already suffered some 5 million casualties – there were we, one of Britain's rare and precious armoured units, still ploughing around, futilely, in the mud of the remote English countryside. It seemed absurd to us, and the absurdity must become apparent to the Allied High Command. We must surely be moved shortly to somewhere where we could at least play some active role.

As time passed, the likelihood of CDL being used became increasingly remote and it was clear to us, as to any thinking person, that the promised 'Second Front' for which the Russians were pressing so strongly, was just not on at this moment. Anyone could see that Britain did not have the resources for anything so ambitious. The only way, it seemed to us, in which CDL could be used was either in checking Rommel in the Western Desert, or in raids on the fortified coasts of Western Europe.

As it happened, shortly after we finally left Penrith, one of these coastal raids, and a very important one for the Allies, took place in the shape of the daring attack on the dock gates at St Nazaire, at the mouth of the Loire. But this was purely a combined naval and commando operation for which CDL could not have been appropriate or useful.

This happened at the end of March 1942, and had a very significant effect on the war at sea. The background was that the mighty German battleship, *Tirpitz*, sister ship of the better known *Bismarck*, was at the time skulking in the Norwegian port of Bergen, waiting a favourable opportunity to join in the highly successful Atlantic U-Boat assault on allied shipping. Her presence might just have made the difference, and it was a pretty fine difference, as to whether our vital trans-Atlantic link was destroyed completely.

The *Tirpitz*, however, required a massive dock to which to retire for repairs and maintenance during her projected Atlantic operations and without such a facility the Germans would not have dared to risk the loss of their last important capital ship. The only suitable dock large enough to accommodate the great ship on the whole Western European coast was that at St Nazaire, which the French had built before the war to accommodate their trans-Atlantic liner *Normandie* which in the 1930s shared the North Atlantic crossing with the British *Queen Mary*.

The theory was that, if the St Nazaire dock could be destroyed, the ability of the Germans to maintain any capital ship in the Atlantic would be destroyed with it and this would spell the end to their use of surface raiders on the convoy routes. Henceforth they would have to depend on the U-Boats alone, and by 1943 the U-Boats had been conquered. So the St Nazaire raid was one of the critical operations of the war. It took the French until 1949 to repair the damage.

The raid was one of the many cases of a combination of daring with successful deception of the enemy. The *Campbeltown* was one of the 50 ageing American destroyers transferred to Britain in return for giving them bases in Bermuda and elsewhere in the West Indies. The idea was that she should be packed with explosives and ram the dock gates, and then, controlled by a time fuse, blow up, completely demolishing the dock. At the same time a Commando group was to be landed and do as much damage as possible to the U-Boat and port facilities generally.

Campbeltown was camouflaged to resemble a German destroyer, enabling her to approach quite closely to the dock gates before the formidable coast defences came into action. When they did, the naval casualties were quite heavy and the Commandos could not be re-embarked and had to be just abandoned to escape individually if they could, via the Spanish border. Sadly, most of them were captured, but a remnant of the naval force, including the commander, returned intact. Meanwhile, *Campbeltown* was left with her explosive-filled belly jammed up against the dock gates. Rather unimaginatively, the German admiral commanding the port boarded the destroyer, accompanied by hundreds of officers and men, but even more surprisingly failed to find the explosives and at 12.35 am the next morning a mighty explosion dealt a death blow to Germany's hitherto highly successful war at sea. Also, 380 Germans in the immediate vicinity were killed – probably exceeding the number of British dead in the raid.

This spectacular success rather went to the heads of the British Combined Operations Command, leading them, quite wrongly, to conclude that a raid in strength even against a strongly fortified port stood a chance of success. The Germans were able to prove the contrary when the ill-fated Dieppe raid was tried in the following October, though Earl Mountbatten, then Chief of Combined Operations, later said, for every man killed at Dieppe, perhaps ten were saved on D-Day, as a result of the experience gained.

All these happenings naturally served to multiply the rumours surrounding the future of our own 11th Battalion, Royal Tank Regiment. As March 1942 approached many of us were granted leave and there was even a rumour at the time that this ought not to have been so, as we were scheduled to be used on an unidentified operation. However, once again nothing happened and finally came the news that we were definitely moving. There was also an indication, wrong as it turned out, that CDL had been scrapped. This was in the shape of a first exercise of 'turrets on, turrets off', which dogged most of the Battalion's existence. We had a brief busy period removing the CDL turrets and replacing them with the original 2-pounder gun turrets for the train journey by tank flats – as, of course, the secret had to be kept and no one was allowed to see the CDL turrets. Even by this time, the 2-pounder gun, and indeed the whole Matilda tank, was hopelessly out-dated.

In the case of the 'Kite', of course, there was also more to it than just changing turrets. There was the business of collecting all her component parts, scattered over Askham Fell, and putting them together again for the journey: a terrific job for the squadron fitters, and a not negligible one for your humble author.

It was clear that we were not immediately going anywhere dangerous, for the destination was revealed as Shorncliffe Barracks, Folkestone, and we were to go there, on tank flats, by train.

Shorncliffe was an old-established and well appointed barracks, with old buildings but laid-on water supplies, a hard-bottomed tank park and roofed-in hangers in which to work among its unheard-of facilities: all luxuries to the 11th who had graduated in the hard school of muddy Penrith. However, we would be entering the front line of the South Coast defences against a still possible German invasion and an increase in discipline was to be expected as the serpent in this Eden. Also I, at least, was reluctant to leave our beloved home which, if mighty uncomfortable, had been essentially happy.

The move turned out to be quite a formidable journey, starting in the wrong direction, as we had first to go back to Carlisle, then were stuck for four and a half hours between Crewe and Stafford because of a derailment, the whole journey taking 18 hours. However, on account of all our NCOs being absent on courses at the time, I was appointed temporary acting Tank Commander of 'Kite' for the journey, my sole and only strictly military distinction of the war. A joke commander of a joke tank.

So ended another episode in my life, a pretty uncomfortable one but nevertheless on the whole enjoyed, for under what other circumstances during wartime would one have been housed in one of England's stately homes, then in the beautiful Lake District and finally in a very superior seaside resort?

3

Shorncliffe – we hinder the defence of southern England and I acquire my one and only war wound

Shorncliffe turned out to be everything that Penrith was not. The camp had been a military establishment from the time of Queen Elizabeth I, when the threat was of invasion from Spain, not Germany, and the buildings we were to inhabit dated from 1860, so the surroundings were hardly modern.

Still, the barrack rooms were large and airy with plenty of windows and, blessing of blessings, 200-watt electric lights. We also had iron bedsteads with adequate space for hanging pegs and lockers, a wooden floor, tables and *chairs*. Attached was a proper washroom with an electric heater which gave warm water – sometimes. There was a good bathhouse with some proper baths, as well as showers, which gave hot water, also sometimes. We had a fireplace but, as the coal shortage was acute, the fire was occasional.

Canteens, most of them good with a fair selection of food, were to be found at every corner and the NAAFI had a radio as blatantly loud as the Penrith effort was feeble. Other facilities included a gymnasium, a garrison church, a sports field and a well equipped kitchen and dining hall which did not stink of stale tea and rotting vegetables. The steam cooking apparatus and clean terrazzo floor effected a veritable improvement in the quality of our food, though this was still hampered by the natural defects of our cooks, who still managed to produce dirty potatoes in spite of having a mechanical potato peeler at their disposal. However, we were able to face meals with a certain relish and very little was now thrown away, in contrast to the 75% waste at Penrith. Reflecting the nation-wide food shortage developing at this stage of the war, there were sometimes complaints as to quantity, in contrast to the earlier superabundance, but deficiencies could still be made up at the numerous canteens.

There was a splendid tank hangar, with concrete floor and electric lights, cutting out the business of the five-mile-distant tank park and its attendant mud, which last fact had incidental advantages like requiring only one guard nightly instead of three, so that 'guards' now occurred only fortnightly.

All these advantages hardly match up to the hotel standards accorded to the present day Army and might be thought to be no more than our due, but hitherto we had enjoyed none of these things.

This military paradise, however, in common with all other paradises, was not without its serpent, and this was so vicious that many of us would rather have been back in Penrith. The snake in this case was personified by the Regimental Sergeant Major and his spate of 'disciplinary measures' such as blancoing ad lib, marching to meals, Adjutant's parades, kit inspections, a magnificently ceremonial guard mounting etc. These kept one in a state of seething exasperation. All this, when we were 22 miles from the enemy's coastline at a time when he might invade at any moment. Most local troops, though fortunately not ourselves this time, still had polished brasses on their equipment, rendering them visible for miles on a sunny day. All this rather negated the limiting of our local bounds to Folkestone and Hythe, or five or six miles of coastline, all of which was barricaded with barbed wire and concrete against invasion. There was even a rumour at one stage that a German patrol had landed and captured intact a complete 'guard' of six men and whisked them off to a German prison camp.

At that time, Folkestone might have qualified as England's new 'depressed area'. Outwardly, it looked much as it had done, with the dignified Georgian architecture appearing as peaceful and permanent as ever with practically no bomb damage apart from the harbour area, and not much there. The pier was wrecked and there were a few sunken fishing boats which no one had bothered to salvage; otherwise one would not have known that it had become a ghost town, almost deserted.

Of shops, not more than one in four remained open, and street after street of apartment and ordinary dwelling houses were empty and shuttered up. Such buildings as remained open were mainly used for billeting troops, whose washing hung from the windows of abandoned hotels. In the streets one saw about twenty servicemen to every civilian, and women were noticeable by their complete absence. Such a contrast to Keswick, where they did not know there was a war on; where they would turn to stare at a soldier and women were thicker than flies in summer.

Yet, in a way, Drake still played bowls at Folkestone, for the place was organised on lavish lines for the troops. There were at least three establishments running dinner and tea dances, three good cinemas, with two more in Hythe, and the local theatre had variety programmes with well known artists.

Our favourite haunt was the Leas Cliff Hall, where there was afternoon, and evening, dancing and sometimes a cabaret. Elegant couples might be seen dancing on the perfect floor in soft light to sweet music. On Sunday nights there was a local talent concert for the troops. One wondered, however, how it came about that the Leas Cliff Hall still had a young and handsome master of ceremonies who had somehow managed to avoid the universal 'call up' for military service.

All this seemed a little like the grand ball at Brussels before the Battle of Waterloo – or perhaps Nero fiddling while Rome burned – and our Squadron cynics also noted that we had a small amount of ammunition stored in our tanks in readiness for invasion, all frightfully correct and warlike – but it seemed that every time we went to the hangar, including the start for the normal morning's work, it was discovered on arrival that we didn't have the key and no one knew who had it. We often waited for twenty minutes to get in.

On this point, one of our lads, a former Sheffield steel worker, provided the perfect comment whilst 'on guard' at some vital place. 'Ah say, thee can't coom in 'ere. Just thee wait while ah gets bullets for this gun and ah'l soon show thee who's master round 'ere.'

Whether this incident had anything to do with it is unknown, but round about the same time war preparedness made an advance in the shape of our being issued with one Bren gun and three Tommy guns per barrack room *with real live ammunition*. I have previously praised the accuracy of the Czech designed Bren (the name came from a collaboration between the Czech town of Brno and the British Enfield Company). I was also impressed with the Tommy gun, a simple weapon free from stoppages* whose only fault was a tendency for the shots to veer high and to the left. It was, of course, of American design, being the gun preferred by Chicago gangsters in the Prohibition days. With any British gun the first thing you learned was the stoppages*, the first one of which was 're-cock and fire' again.

---

* Stoppages: something the wretched gun does to the unfortunate gunner. He will be firing merrily away and suddenly it will stop and he will have no indication as to why.

Also round about this time I was feeling particularly fed up with the day's activities and was heard to declare publicly that I almost wished Jerry would drop a bomb on the place and blow the whole shoot to glory. I must have been exercising my psychic strain for, so help me, that very evening the Luftwaffe did just that!

I was shaving in the washroom when I heard the familiar old 'whee-boomph' of falling bombs. I went on shaving, eventually returning to the barrack room to find everyone emerging gingerly from under their beds. It turned out that three small bombs, probably 25 pounders, from captured British stocks taken at Dunkirk, hit C Squadron tank hangar. One was a direct hit on the Colonel's car, which does not live here any more, and another blew some plates out of a steel door. However, the encouraging feature was that the third one burst immediately in front of one of our tanks which was absolutely undamaged apart from a small dent in the two pounder gun.

This lined up with my subsequent conclusion that in this war you paid your money and took your choice. For preference, you would not be in a tank at all; you were safer in the infantry, where you could at least get to ground instead of being a sitting target.

But if you had to be in a tank, then you could have a British tank, which was as safe as any tank could be at that time, but was absolutely guaranteed to break down about every third mile covered. Or you could have an American tank, which was reasonably reliable mechanically, but might as well have been made of cardboard for all the protection it gave. The casualty rate among the American Shermans in the later European campaign abundantly proved the latter conclusion, while we were shortly to demonstrate the former, ourselves, in our warlike exercises at Shorncliffe.

One night we had a pukka invasion scare. Some troops of another unit on night manoeuvres wearing Balaclava helmets were taken for German parachutists and the alarm was given. I was out at the time but was given to understand that our camp defences were ready, with everyone standing by, in good time. No one knew how it came about, but presumably it was just another case of lack of co-ordination between units. The local infantry were evidently out on manoeuvres and rumour had it that we were shortly to join them.

At this stage, someone decided that it would be a good idea if we were to have some firing practise with our two pounder tank guns. As previously mentioned, the two pounder was a very good little gun, but with the emphasis on the 'little'. The projectile was just not heavy enough, and it was being replaced by the six pounder. The cliffs behind the coast here were selected as a suitable baffle for our fire and we had the satisfaction for the first time of firing live ammunition – proving that the gun really did work and was not just for taking to pieces and oiling yet again. Some of us, regardless of our satisfaction at firing something heavier than a ·303 round, were nevertheless a bit doubtful at the wisdom of 'targeting' the cliff face. Remembering our preliminary training on the solitary two pounder, borrowed from the Imperial War Museum, we knew about its high muzzle velocity of 2,650 feet per second and were a little worried about ricochets: with only too good reason, for the proceedings were summarily halted when the RAF at Hawkinge furiously protested that we had damaged two of their precious Spitfires, then resting peacefully on the airfield, on which the salvation of the nation had depended back in 1940! Indeed, it was fortunate that Hitler did not know that the 11th Battalion, Royal Tank Regiment were part of the coastal defences at this point.

However, despite such bungled attempts at serious training, most of the time was still spent in 'maintaining' the tanks. This, in the case of Kite, meant that she was still out of action: indeed some of the odd bits in which she had arrived from Penrith had still not been assembled. At this stage she suffered from a fuel leak, a broken spindle in one bogey and mud in the final drive casing. We were later to hear more about final drives, with the trouble not confined to mud in the casing. Meanwhile rumours again spread that we were shortly due for another move, making it necessary that all tanks, even Kite, should be 'on the road'.

Leave became due again, but it was only 24 hours this time, which made it impractical for me to travel home to the Midlands, where they had experienced real war during the 'blitz' on the Birmingham area. A house opposite to my home and not 100 yards away had been completely demolished and an enormous crater, some 60 feet wide, had appeared on the golf course just behind our house where a 1,000 pound bomb, probably intended for the Dunlop tyre factory or the nearby aircraft factory, had hopelessly missed its target, so showing that military incompetence was by no means confined to our side.

Fortunately, our military incompetence was more than compensated for by the brilliance of our scientists. A really effective raid on the only plant in all Britain that had the capacity to produce tyres on the enormous scale required for a war that moved almost entirely on wheels, could well have altered the whole course of the conflict and the future of civilisation. 'But for the grace of God' could have been Hitler's epitaph. He so nearly made it.

His failure was due to a scientific triumph. The Luftwaffe had the benefit of their own admittedly brilliant scientists, who had devised a direction-finding beam. Two of these beams the aircraft were supposed to follow until they intersected over the intended target. But they had reckoned without a previously unknown scientist at Birmingham University, who was a contemporary of my own brother there. This scientist devised a means of bending the direction-finding beam so that the bombs fell, not on the target, but near to our house in Sutton Coldfield, or among the wilds of Sutton Park. He might well have won the war for us, his achievement only being surpassed by the code-breakers who made possible the gigantic deception practised on the Germans, whereby they were completely deceived as to where the D-Day invasion was to take place.

But to return to the subject of leave. As it was impossible for me to get home for a 24 hour leave from Shorncliffe, I opted instead, to my regret, for a return visit to Canterbury to renew old memories. One should never, ever, do this, for the place is never as one remembers it and has usually deteriorated.

Canterbury had not yet suffered the Baedeker raids in which the Luftwaffe attacked Britain's ancient cultural heritage, having failed both to destroy its industry and to terrorise its civilian population. In these, the whole north eastern section of the little city (population then about 23,000) was flattened, and permanently damaged by post-war red brick rebuilding, completely out of keeping with the stone-built original. Could this Baedeker barbarity have helped to trigger off one of the disgraces later in the war, one of the RAF's few discreditable actions, the destruction of the historic German city of Dresden?

Fortunately, the Luftwaffe made a mess of their cultural destruction, for they missed nearly all of the historically important areas in Canterbury, including the Cathedral, the very foundation of Christianity in England. What they *did* destroy, ironically, was the former brothel area north of Butchery Lane, which in my schooldays was a strictly prohibited area.

I went first to the Cathedral, which was actually much as I left it. The Gatehouse had been improved, having been restored and repainted in its original medieval colours. But the interior indeed showed the marks of war. All the tombs had been sandbagged up and a considerable amount of glass broken. In particular, the Kings School Chapel, where I had spent many a tranquil hour, seated behind the helmet, armour and even the tatters of his surcoat hanging from a nail, of the Black Prince, the greatest warrior of his day, was barred off and filled with debris. It transpired that the school had been evacuated to St Austell in Cornwall, but its buildings, horror of horrors, had been transformed into a *barracks*. The Cathedral Green was being used for football, the Cloister buildings were a dining hall and the War Memorial steps were chipped and broken. Only the Norman staircase of the historic monuments had escaped damage. The main body of the classrooms were a decontamination centre, the prefects' studies offices, and the tuck shop an ammunition store. And the crowning desecration of them all, the Parry Library, my solace and sanctuary from the storms of life during my schooldays, was a British Restaurant – dinners 6d and 9d. Looking back on my outrage at this time from the viewpoint of the 1990s, what now strikes me is that there was a time when one could actually get an edible meal for 6d and 9d.

The last, unkindest, cut of all during the 1980s visit was to find that the School, only about 280 strong in my day, had been expanded to some 700 and now included Sixth Form Girls. Several new houses had been added – but how could this ancient institution, the oldest school in Britain and perhaps in the world, founded by St Augustine, no less, the founder of Christianity in southern Britain, be so lacking in a feeling of the fitness of things? They had added another house, by putting up a hideous modern building in the ancient Mint Yard, site of the first Royal Mint in England. At least the wartime vandals did one thing appropriately: the old city's only surviving city gate, The Westgate, had been returned to its original medieval function. It was again a watch tower.

As it turned out, this leave was to be the last, at home, for a long time; for 'schemes' as the exercises were called, became more frequent and 'Kite' was 'on the road', or actually working, for all of them. Admittedly, she broke down each time, early in the proceedings, and arrived home last. Still, we got her there and back, and I was filled with justifiable pride. It actually appeared that I, the world's worst man with machinery, was on the way to mastering so perverse and cantankerous an engine as 'Kite'.

We did several night approach marches, yet another way of doing one out of one's sleep, road runs of 50 miles or so and one mock battle in co-operation with an infantry brigade. For this last, some 40 of our total of 60 tanks were in action. Spitfires carried out preparatory dive bombing, and artillery laid down a smoke screen for us to operate under. Quite the real thing in theory, but marred by side-splitting anachronisms like Generals in full regalia galloping about the place on their thoroughbred chargers.

Each tank, and other units, had with it an 'umpire' who ruled who was knocked out, and when and why. 'Kite', needlessly to say, under the charge of Peter, our troop officer, ran into a minefield and was ruled 'out of action' before she had travelled 100 yards. We dutifully hung out our red and yellow 'out of action' flag. However, it seemed that the Spitfire pilot opposing us had not been told what this meant for, apparently under the impression that we were brigade headquarters, or some such thing, singled out 'Kite' for attacks and dived at us for ten minutes or more, providing the best aerial show I had ever seen.

The whole affair would have been most enjoyable if we had not had a spate of trouble with 'Kite'. We had had trouble with one engine fan on the approach march, and the driver and I had spent one and a half hours from the unearthly hour of 5 am fixing up the coupling, just finishing in time for the attack. As soon as all was over, the fan conked out again and we appeared to be marooned. However, our consort, 'Thrush', had also conked out so it was decided to make one fit tank out of two wrecks by cannibalisation. So I took out their good fan and transferred it to 'Kite'. Of course, the damn thing did not fit and I fiddled about for hours. When we finally did get going, the repair still fouled the Rackham steering clutch, causing further trouble. We finally arrived home five hours after everyone else. Still, we *got* there and the work was about 80% mine.

In another 'scheme' realism was added to the proceedings by our tanks advancing against genuine Bren gun fire. 'Kite', of course, became stuck, nose downwards, in the first stream to be crossed and became an excellent target for the Bren gunners. The driver paid for his inability to see the ditch through his periscope by spending twenty minutes in his closed compartment, under water, before we could get 'Kite' towed out. Surprisingly we were not hit once by the opposing fire. Perhaps this is the feature that most impresses the soldier undergoing his baptism of fire; how so few people can possibly be hit by such a multitude of missiles. I believe it was officially reckoned at the time that it took the expenditure of an average of 5,000 rounds of ammunition to cause one casualty. This gives some idea of the terrific supply problem of a modern army.

Another 'scheme', a night approach march involving a pontoon bridge crossing of the tiny river Stour, also ended in farce, for unfortunately the Stour developed a 'bore' which washed the bridges away.

As a particularly beautiful Spring came to an end, rumours, this time correct, again proliferated that we were shortly to be involved in a really grand 'scheme', involving a whole army, and that this would involve our leaving Shorncliffe and moving to Worthing for a period. Some said that, from Worthing, we should be moving to my beloved Scotland, but this last prediction turned out to be very wide of the mark, for our comfortable stay in the South of England was about to end, for me rather spectacularly.

The projected exercise, this time, turned out to be the one in which the, later, Field Marshal Montgomery, was first tried out as an Army Commander, so it was really important. The 11th Battalion, Royal Tank Regiment were to be part of a supposed invading force, based on Shorncliffe, attacking the defending force, based on Worthing. We, with our antique Matildas, were opposed by a battalion of the then brand-new 'Churchill' tanks, being tried out in action for the first time. So, there followed a grand stripping of tanks, with this time, not only 'Kite', but the entire battalion lying in pieces all over the tank hangar. Needless to say, it was expected that the Battalion should be at full strength, and everyone, including even 'Kite', was required to be 'on the road'.

And here follows the sorry tale of how your humble author almost wrecked an important Army exercise – and paid a penalty for it.

The Matilda was a diesel engined tank, so its oil filter was an important engine component. We were instructed to take out the oil filters and wash them in paraffin and, of course, 'Kite' objected to being submitted to this indignity. Possibly influenced by the absurdity of this procedure, Trooper Wilson, M.W. No. 7931904, duly made a mess of the operation. Having washed the oil filter, he proceeded to screw it back in position, but as usual being without any sympathetic feeling for mechanical things, and at that time being too damned strong, over-tightened the central spindle by which it was attached – in fact, tightened it to the point of stripping the thread.

Hesitantly I took the wrecked oil filter to the fitter sergeant. 'Look, Sergeant, what I've done.' 'Oh my God,' he replied, 'we haven't got another of those in the Squadron stores.' Nor had they in Battalion stores, nor in Brigade or Divisional stores. In fact, it took three days, during which the exercise was held up, to locate an oil filter somewhere in the north of Scotland. I cannot imagine General Montgomery, who, absolutely contrary to Army tradition, expected things actually to work – and this was the secret of his success – being over pleased at the delay. I have never understood how it was that I was not placed on a charge for my effective piece of wrecking. But that, again, was then the British Army: have a dirty cap badge and you were automatically placed on a charge: hold up the most important Army exercise since the evacuation of Dunkirk and you got away with it Scot free.

However, eventually a replacement filter was obtained from somewhere and the delayed exercise could begin. As always, of course, it had to be a night attack – thereby once again depriving one of a night's sleep – and what a night it turned out to be – probably the worst of my entire long life.

Memories are confused, but we seemed to spend most of the night passing, and re-passing through the village of Tenderden. Needless to say, at an early stage 'Kite' started to play up, showing from the temperature gauge an over-heating engine – something totally inadmissible. For allowing a tank engine to overheat, one would certainly be put on a charge. As I believe I explained previously, the real job of the tank's wireless operator was to do all the odd jobs that arose: in this case to lift the three heavy hinged louvres covering the engine compartment and inspect the water system. As soon as I unscrewed the cap, it was obvious what was wrong, for it gave off quite a quantity of steam, so I had to find a source of water before we could proceed further – and water in considerable quantity, at that. I found some in a village pond, passing it in bucketfulls up to Kite's engine compartment. So we were off again and must have proceeded all of a couple of miles before the temperature gauge again registered the need for water. This time, I had to knock up a cottager in the middle of the night in order to find any. And so we continued throughout the night, having to stop every two or three miles to find pond, village pump or understandably grumpy cottager. I was, at this time, a fit young man in my prime, but out of condition from having done no heavy work since joining the Army. The watering of 'Kite' involving finding the source of water, moving it uphill by the bucketfull on to the high rear end of 'Kite' and, each time, lifting and replacing the armour plate louvres which must have weighed the best part of a hundredweight, was indeed a job for a strong man.

So, by the time most welcome dawn lighted the eastern sky I was in a pretty exhausted condition. And what was the first thing we saw? It would appear that our side had unquestionably won our mini-war, for there, drawn up neatly by the side of the road, was the whole battalion of the Churchill tanks opposing us – every one of them 'off the road'. Of course, at the time we were mystified at this unaccountable collapse of the opposition, but it subsequently transpired that there was a fundamental design fault in the Churchill tank, for the final drives of the entire battalion had stripped during their night manoeuvrings – the ideal time for Hitler to have invaded if only he had known!

So there was now nothing to prevent our triumphal advance on Worthing, as 'Kite' approached her final trial: climbing the escarpment of the South Downs prior to entering the town. She made it, but was evidently at her last gasp, as I was, when we reached the summit.

I was leaning, gratefully, against her side thinking that my ordeal was over and with no idea that I was about to acquire my one and only war wound. But I had counted without my friend, Myers, who was just about as mechanically inept as I was. He selected this moment, seeing that I was 'hors de combat', to lift the louvres again to inspect the water cap. Poor old 'Kite', after climbing the escarpment turned out to have no water left in her system, but plenty of scalding steam. The moment the water cap was released she emitted a powerful jet which hit me, leaning against the side of the tank, slap in the side of the face. Needless to say I suffered a severe scald, both on the face and down the left side of the body.

Fortunately for me, we were within twenty minutes' run of our final destination in the town centre of Worthing and, 'Kite' having again been suitably 'watered' by someone else, I was duly delivered to the squadron medical officer, who, as previously recorded, was a vet before the war, but who coped most admirably with my emergency. Being in a state of shock, I remember almost nothing of the final leg of that journey.

I must have sustained a very severe scald and was quite expecting to be marked for life; but not a bit of it. The MO treated my face with gentian violet and the less severe body burns with tannic acid, and for the following fortnight I was the sight of Worthing, with my bright purple face. No doubt my treatment would now be regarded as completely out of date, but it worked like a charm and, incidentally, the scalds healed without a trace.

There followed a brief idyllic period when we were quartered in requisitioned private houses in Worthing. There was no furniture and we slept on the floor, but this last time on English soil – though at the time we were not to know this – was perhaps the most comfortable of my whole five years' Army service. We were left to ourselves.

Meanwhile, the rumour mill ground and it was clear that we were shortly bound for somewhere and, all too soon, we found ourselves again at the town station loading our tanks, including 'Kite', on to railway flat cars, and ourselves into a troop train. This proved to be a long and complicated journey, and admittedly remarkably well camouflaged, for we visited all kinds of unlikely places in eastern England before waking one morning to find ourselves in what was clearly a dock area, and turned out to be Glasgow's port of Greenock. Here the dockers greeted us with ill-concealed sympathy tinged with derision, on noting that we were equipped with the out-dated Matilda tank with its wretched little two-pounder gun. They would indeed have been surprised had they known the truth of our mission.

4

The 11th Battalion goes to sea

The next morning was, appropriately, a beautiful one as we made our way out of Greenock and down the Clyde towards the open sea, the hills of Argyll showing up magnificently against the early morning sky; the Kyles of Bute passing close on the starboard side, before we joined a large convoy assembling off the Isle of Islay. It became clear that we were probably due for a long voyage but, at this stage one could only guess as to where. None of us realised, I think, at this time that this would be our last glimpse of Britain for two whole years, until early in 1944. It seemed logical that we must be bound for the Middle East, but at first this seemed to be in doubt.

I can't remember the number of ships assembled in the North Channel facing the open Atlantic, but it must have been considerable for we had an escort of six destroyers and one ancient cruiser. And here was one of many recurring patterns repeating themselves throughout my long life. For the cruiser was no other than the *Hawkins*, immediately recognisable to me from my schooldays in China, when she was the flagship of the British China Squadron which formed part of the international flotilla stationed off shore from the sea front at Chefoo.

Hawkins, like a mother hen marshalling her chicks, duly assembled the convoy into the formation she wanted and we set off into the blue, to our surprise and mystification, heading due west out into the Atlantic. But this was only a ploy, intended to fool not us, but the U-Boat commanders, to whom this large convoy must have seemed an ideal target, during a period when U-Boat activity was at its height.

Our convoy, spread over miles and miles of ocean, must have presented a splendid sight and, credit to the Navy and RAF, was certainly being shepherded with care. An early incident, for which I never learned the true explanation, was when a Sunderland flying boat, flying very low, was circling the convoy, presumably having spotted a U-Boat, when it suddenly dived straight into the sea and was not seen again. I was watching carefully at the time, but saw no indication of hostile fire to account for this incident, from which the flying boat's crew must unfortunately have died. Just one more of the war's unexplained minor tragedies.

Of course, the early part of our voyage was taken up mainly with getting to know our new floating home, and coming to terms with its living conditions. We were used to being uncomfortable, but our troopship was something else again. She was a medium sized cargo ship, of some 10,000 tons, which had been gutted to accommodate three layers of troop decks. She carried a few passengers, and what remained of the original passenger accommodation was, of course, devoted to the officers, while no fewer than 4,000 troops were crammed into the troop decks below. The sleeping conditions were sheer hell and, in retrospect, apart from our not being chained, could not have been much better than those of the negro slaves transported to America during the 17th and 18th centuries. Admittedly, I could not have spoken to more than a tiny proportion of this vast number of men, but what now surprises me most is that I never, once, heard anyone complain about the conditions. There seemed to be universal acceptance of the fact that this was the way things were in wartime; no one could do a thing about it and there was no point in holding anyone to blame, let alone making things even worse by organising a protest.

To get such numbers aboard a ship of this size, the troop decks had to have pretty low ceilings. The men slept in three layers, the fortunate ones had hammocks slung, naval style, from the pipework above; the less fortunate had the top of the dining tables below and the really unfortunate were on the greasy floor among the inedible scraps, etc. from the last meal. Of course, it was our own responsibility to try to keep this hell hole as clean and salubrious as possible, but it was an impossible task and the state of the atmosphere, packed almost like sardines as we were, when we later entered the tropics and crossed the equator, can be imagined. During the daytime we were, of course, allowed on deck, but here it was hardly less uncomfortable, for the space was so limited that there was room only for everyone to sit, if all pulled their knees right up under their chins. So, one could stand on deck or sit in the manner described, but any kind of movement was almost impossible. The unnatural sitting position, and general lack of opportunity for exercise, meant that when we finally did get an opportunity to go ashore, many men had the tendons in their legs so drawn up that they had difficulty in walking normally.

Again, in retrospect, one is amazed that everyone seemed to survive these conditions and I heard of no cases of serious illness resulting. Perhaps, mercifully, I can't even remember how we managed for sanitary arrangements, though I do remember the unpleasantness of shaving in sea water. In my own case, a tough and unpleasant childhood had prepared me for this ordeal, and no doubt many of the lads came from homes so poor that they were used to hardship. My mind goes back to Trooper Grayson, who had never experienced having a change of clothing.

Eventually we did turn south, into what seemed a more logical direction and, of course, as we entered tropical waters, our floating prison began to heat up, particularly at night on the overcrowded troop decks, which were soon absolutely stinking, despite all efforts to keep them as clean as possible, when crammed with so many bodies.

Eventually we reversed direction completely, turning to the east towards the coast of West Africa and the steaming port of Freetown in Sierra Leone. The sight of Freetown's extensive open harbour with its verdant green hills backing it was very welcome and we hoped that we might be able to go ashore here, and stretch our cramped legs – but not so. This was evidently only a brief stop for refuelling and we saw no more of West Africa than some magnificently muscled black African stevedores.

So, back to sea and steadily southwards, in our increasing discomfort, towards the Equator, where some attempt was made to conduct the time-honoured Father Neptune ceremony. By this time, the danger of U-Boats was held to have diminished, for a large part of the convoy's escort left us. The brilliant northern stars disappeared to be replaced by the, to my mind, disappointing southern sky, dominated by the Southern Cross. The oppressive heat diminished as the fresh southerly winds took over and massive seas imposed their own pattern of suffering. Sea sickness was added to our discomforts.

Doubt as to our destination was finally settled when we ran into the huge rollers marking approach to the Cape of Good Hope and the southern tip of Africa. We could not now be headed for anywhere but the battle zones of the Middle East. But even this assumption proved to be only partially correct.

Surely no sailors every longed more for dry land than we did when, one evening, the magnificent silhouette of Table Mountain broke the monotony of the horizon, bursting into the myriad twinkling lights of Cape Town as dusk developed.

For me, this was probably the most heartening sight of the whole war. Everyone in Britain had become depressed by the very necessary 'blackout' during the long hours of darkness, when to show a light of any kind was the ultimate crime, threatening the whole community. No one had seen an artificial light out of doors for nearly three years, beyond the tiny slits which were all that were allowed as a vehicle's headlights. We of the 11th Battalion RTR had suffered more than most from this deprivation of light from our long period of night exercises at Penrith and our particularly dimly lit living conditions whilst there. Imagine the wonder of approaching again a fully lit city with Cape Town's magnificent setting.

Docking completed, we hoped above everything that here we would be allowed ashore to stretch our legs and enter into this festival of light. For once, we were not disappointed, though we soon found that the South African authorities had taken due precautions to see that their beautiful city was not disrupted by unruly troops suddenly released from their prison-like troopship.

As each party descended the ship's gangway the following morning they were met by some sort of civic delegation who had undertaken to entertain us, under supervision, for the duration of our visit. With one companion, I did manage one independent trip into the surrounding countryside offering an opportunity to stretch our bodies again. During the afternoon we escaped into the hilly country surrounding the city for an orgy of climbing and rushing headlong down steep slopes.

Making our way back to the quay, we were collected again by the reception organisers and taken on to a formal dinner at a local hotel. To eat civilian food again under civilised conditions was to me sheer heaven, though I fear that many of our lads, particularly those from poor homes in West Yorkshire, or the later consignment from Tyneside, were a bit overwhelmed by the occasion. Once again, I found myself fulfilling the function of 'Father' of B Squadron by showing dinner neighbours who had never attended a formal dinner before which of the array of cutlery to use for each course. Again, one is struck by how much the social scene has changed between the 1940s and the 1990s.

After dinner we were taken on to a concert with an opera singer giving a spirited rendering from *Pagliacci*. Again, I fear that a section of this audience were out of their depth, though there were noisy interruptions not from us, but from among the locals. Nevertheless, as we returned to our prison ship that night, I think there were few who did not appreciate their brief release from captivity into the light and hospitality of Cape Town.

So back to the stormy seas around the Cape of Good Hope to resume our long voyage, with not another glimpse of land until we approached the Gulf of Aden. The Indian Ocean was quieter than the South Atlantic and it was not too long before the temperature again began to climb, with our misery steadily increasing as we approached the Equator for the second time. Though this was not officially allowed, I was among those who risked sleeping on deck rather than in the hell hole below.

The hottest and most unpleasant part of the voyage, however, was still to come, though we were by now reasonably clear of the U-Boat menace and no longer needed escorts. Surely one of the most forbidding spots on earth, must be the black rocks heralding the port of Aden, which I imagine was one part of the former British Empire which the British troops garrisoning it would have been most glad to be rid of. No one, I think, particularly regretted not being allowed ashore at Aden, for all realised that we must be nearing our final destination, which we still thought must be the Western Desert fighting front.

During the final stage of our voyage up the Red Sea, and the Gulf of Suez, there were occasional glimpses of land, and everyone's prime wish after our seven weeks at sea was just to set foot on dry land again. There might have been less enthusiasm if we had known that the dry land was to consist only of shifting sand, for almost two years.

As our men staggered ashore at Suez, trying to regain the use of their legs, they were not over pleased to be bundled smartly into railway cattle trucks dating from the 1914-18 war, labelled 'Hommes 40 Chevaux 14', for another very unpleasant journey across the Sinai Desert, to what was then the southern part of Palestine. Visions of the Western Desert battlefront, whether welcomed or not, began to fade, as we de-trained at the port of Gaza and set off, by motor transport, eastwards across the desert, finally to be dumped in what seemed to us to be more desert, but which we later learned was considered by the local Arabs to be comparatively fertile land. We had arrived.

5

The era of B Squadron 'Corpse' in the Holy Land

We had arrived at Rafah, which was of absolutely no significance in our war, but important in a later and lesser war. This was the precise spot where the Israeli-Arab Six Day War of 1967 was to commence.

For us, this could have been the most boring and uneventful of all our locations, but in B Squadron, we contrived – that is some of us did, to make it into a quite rewarding exercise. For what the few intellectuals in the Squadron did was nothing less than to reorganise our otherwise totally inactive unit on civilian lines, effectively ignoring the uncomfortable fact that we were in the Army.

Just out of sight was the small Arab town of Khan Yunis, but this made no impact at all on us. We were dumped in what seemed to be a featureless patch of desert, isolated from all other forms of life. There were two solitary palm trees breaking opposite horizons but nothing whatever else to catch the eye. The surface was soft, shifting sand which fell away under one's feet, causing us to long just for solid ground. It was significant that the Squadron's usual PT enthusiasts rapidly decided that PT was no longer appropriate at Rafah: the men had quite enough exercise in just getting around on the sand.

Shortly we were to have yet more evidence of traditional military thinking bending itself to local conditions. Of course, the first thought occurring to the military mind was ease of supply to this isolated unit, to which the inevitable conclusion was to build a road from the supply port to our camp. Bearing in mind that the route lay entirely over sand with no foundation underneath, I can only leave it to those better qualified to judge between whether this project was wildly optimistic or, as it appears to me, stark, staring mad. Anyway, what was done was just to lay a strip of tarmac directly on to the sand. Obviously, I would have thought, this started to break up almost as soon as it was laid and in the course of a week or so had disintegrated completely. Somehow, we were evidently kept in essential supplies without the aid of a road.

One aspect of the local environment the military mind never came to terms with was the daily sandstorm, which came with monotonous regularity at about 1.00 pm every day. This naturally clashed with lunchtime. Upon our arrival, the first semi-permanent erection was the large marquee which served as a dining hall. This gave some slight protection against the elements, but not nearly enough to keep out a Rafah sandstorm. So throughout our two-year stay, the regular procedure was to collect one's meal from the food queue, then scrape the layer of sand from the top of the meal before attempting to eat it. This could not be anything but a very rough and incomplete procedure and we must have ingested vast quantities of sand in the course of our long stay at Rafah. Small wonder that towards the end of my war service I had developed a duodenal ulcer, which eventually led to my early discharge as medical Category C2.

Shortly after our arrival a further depressing event was the separate arrival of our tanks, so I found myself re-united with the detested 'Kite' – still without any replacement engine. Gloom was heightened by the further separate arrival of our CDL turrets. So, once again, we went through the routine of changing turrets, putting paid for good to any chance of our being used as a fighting unit. Presumably, the turrets and their 2-pounder guns would eventually have been melted down for scrap.

So, we resumed where we had left off at Penrith, but without Penrith's flesh pots and, even more important for many, without Penrith's superb beer. We came to realise how relatively well off we had been in that slough of rain and mud compared with the present ubiquitous sand and the total lack of anything to do.

During the day we continued to clean and polish the tanks and periodically to take them to pieces yet again, as sand got into the final drives or a track broke, etc. 'Kite', in accordance with her past history, was in pieces as often as she was 'on the road' or, more accurately, 'on the sand'. During the summer of 1942 the Middle East sun blazed down with all its power on our tank park, but everyone 'worked' stripped to the waist wearing only their berets on their heads and with the full power of the sun on the backs of their necks. Yet I never heard of a single case of sunstroke. We had duly been issued, as all troops in the Middle East were, with sun helmets which were promptly dumped in a central store in Cairo, where there were reported to be upwards of a million of them. Yet another example of colossal wartime waste, based on ignorant pre-war misconceptions.

During the nights, and every night, we continued to be deprived of our sleep by the never ending night exercises, in which the desert calm continued to be pierced by our flashing lights. Thankfully, there was no one there to observe them but a group of the local Bedouin, who apparently thought this was some kind of a show, staged for their special benefit. They would squat on the ground in a solemn circle waiting for the night's entertainment to begin.

We, of course, were only too conscious of the permanent pressure from Churchill every time the 8th Army became bogged down – which was pretty often – to use our CDL to make a breakthrough. And this threat continued until Montgomery's breakthrough at Alamein in 1943, which was achieved, yet again, without our help. After Alamein, we thought that our boring inactivity must surely have come to an end, but right up to 1944, the concept of CDL still remained alive.

So, as time went by, our desert camp became more and more permanent. At first our tents, one to a troop, were just pitched on the ground in the normal manner. Then it was discovered that there was better protection from the sandstorms if they were dug into the ground to tent wall level, leaving only the roof exposed to the elements. This arrangement made further refinements possible, like a locker space being cut out of the sand wall, so that each of us now had a private space for storing our personal things. It might not be believed today but at the time this was, to us, the height of luxury.

The individual tents became, despite the Army pressure for uniformity, more and more personalised, even to the point of having a 'house name' at the entrance. Mine was called 'Crook's Nook', after Lt Peter Crook, our very inadequate Troop Officer, who was surely an even worse soldier than I was. The lettering of the name was devised by myself, using knowledge acquired from my father as an architect. It was was of a particularly obscure design, which it was beyond the powers of the inspecting officer to decipher, so it was left undisturbed.

Sundry corrugated iron sheds also began appearing, as the process of civilisation began to spread over the site. There was the lecture shed, where public meetings of various kinds were held, the well patronised Squadron Library and eventually the so called EPP House. I cannot remember what the letters stood for. This centre for intellectual study contained war maps showing the progress both of our own forces and those of the then popular 'Uncle Joe' Stalin. We recorded not only the great victory of Alamein, but the huge tank battle at Kursk where the Russian T34 tanks finally broke the hitherto invincible German Panzers. Here also we had our own wall newspaper, in the compilation of which another fondly remembered figure, Sergeant Bill Purver, a peacetime local government officer, and I were the principal agents.

These developments led to a certain division of the squadron into the intellectuals and the football oriented majority, headed by one corporal Ramsden, formerly a Rugby League professional. However, even the footballers had to admit that it was I who, by common consent, had the best body in the Squadron, despite being a wearer of glasses, being then still short-sighted.

But I think it was the British sense of humour, before everything else, that preserved sanity during this so uneventful period. My own contribution to this was the creation of an alter persona for myself, dubbed 'B Squadron Corpse' who naturally lived in 'The Morgue', the alternative name for our tent. There follows a contemporary account entitled 'A Day in the Life of B Squadron Corpse' which conveys the general idea. The 'Corpse' little thought at the time that he would survive to age 84, probably outlasting most of his Army contemporaries.

Just a Day in the Life of B Squadron 'Corpse'

Reveille. As first light tinges the eastern skies the Orderly Sergeant does his rounds awakening the NCOs i/c tents. These gentlemen grumble sleepily and, in some cases, as they are supposed to do, proceed to arouse their tents forthwith. NCO i/c 'The Morgue' calls everyone, including the 'Corpse' who naturally does not even hear him.
Reveille plus 15 mins. NCO i/c 'Morgue' returning from wash, calls 'Corpse' again, who stirs uneasily in his sleep, rolls over and back into the arms of Morpheus.
Reveille plus 30 mins. NCO i/c 'Morgue', his patience wearing thin (for you must remember this sort of thing happens every morning), summons Corpse in stentorian voice telling him it is breakfast time. Corpse grunts and says he is coming; NCO gives it up as a bad job and departs to breakfast. Corpse continues to lie in dazed condition.
Reveille plus 40 mins. Conviction that he must get up having finally penetrated Corpse's befuddled brain, he gets out, has hurried wash

and looks for eating utensils. Eventually finds utensils partly on floor and partly on someone else's bed. Staggers off to breakfast. (All this is done, you must clearly understand, still in his sleep). Corpse tacks on to end of half-mile long queue and resumes his slumbers, eventually getting served from the last revolting dregs from the bottom of the pans. Proceeds to eat breakfast hurriedly. Glancing at watch, suddenly remembers it is 20 minutes slow, bolts remainder of food, and dashes back. On arrival back finds rest of tent donning overalls ready for parade, which he is informed is due to take place in 10 minutes time. Proceeds methodically to get dressed and make up bed.

Blast of Orderly Sergeant's whistle rends the air, which brings home to Corpse with jolt that he is on fatigues today, and so on parade 10 minutes earlier, or to be precise – *now*. Goes into flat spin and, amid a whirl of arms, legs, clothing and utensils, gets self from underpants into overalls, bed from chaos into fit state for inspection, all in a matter of about 10 seconds. Arriving on Parade Ground still doing up buttons and bootlaces, suddenly realises has forgotten beret. Tears back, while parade patiently waits, turns tent upside down again to discover missing head-gear, and arrives back not more than a minute after the original whistle. Finding with surprise and relief that contrary to all the laws of reason he had 'made it' again, our moribund friend subsides into his usual tempo and is marched off to his duties.

About 10.00 hours. Corpse recovers consciousness sufficiently to be able to return the greetings of his friends and, running into one George Gray, the 'Sub-Corpse', his pupil and satellite, greets him in the usual manner of members of the select 'Corpse Club', with the thumbs-down sign and the words 'Roll on Death'. 'Corpse' expresses doubt to the 'Sub-Corpse' as to whether he will last the day out. 'Sub-Corpse' thinks he will, and maintains that, anyway, he, the 'Sub-Corpse', is in far worse shape. To save argument, the Corpse passes the point, though far from being in agreement with it, and suggests that the Sub-Corpse should perform his obvious duty as pupil to master, and carry him over to break. Sub-Corpse retaliates by suggesting that he is in need of a like service himself, so we compromise by supporting each other.

Over the cup of faintly lemon-tinged water which the NAAFI optimistically passes off as lemonade, the Sub-Corpse asks the Corpse what he intends to talk about at his lecture to the Thursday

Club that night. The Corpse replies that he has not even got round to thinking about it yet, and realises that he had better 'get thinking' without further delay.

Panting in the mounting heat and sweating profusely, the Corpse staggers back to his duties, meanwhile sorting out in his now approximately awakened mind the things it is incumbent upon him to do this day. Skipping a few of the more obvious difficulties, such as how he is to manage to be on three parades at one and the same time that afternoon; he finds that he has to arrange for a librarian for duty that night, prepare his EPP exhibit, draw a map to illustrate the latter, assist in the re-erection of EPP House recently moved, do some cataloguing at the Library, clean his equipment in preparation for 'guard' the next night, bundle up and label his washing, and deliver promised lecture at Thursday Club that night. In his 'spare time' he also reflects that it would be desirable to have a shower, a hair-cut, and do some of the washing he was too busy to parcel up for the laundry last week.

11.00 hours. The Corpse's cogitations are interrupted at the dirtiest and most unsuitable stage of his morning's work by arrival of the Education and Welfare Officer for a conflab on various matters concerning EPP, the Library, the Thursday Club, etc. On being informed that the Corpse has had no time to attend to any of the matters in question, E & WO shows a tendency to 'flap'. He is duly soothed and assured that all will yet be well in the hands of the Corpse, the Sub-Corpse and various satellites – (God and the Squadron Authorities willing).

12.00 hours. Supported by little but the thickness of the atmosphere as it is now as usual at this time beginning to blow sand, the Corpse drags himself off to lunch and hitches on to the customary queue, right in line with all the smuts from the cookhouse. Sadly reflects that he is making himself still more washing standing in that unpropitious spot.

12.30. hours. Having absorbed as much of his lunch as the flies have left him, the Corpse washes up in the oozing slime provided for this purpose, and proceeds to his siesta, which is the period in which he usually reckons to clear up most of his necessary work. Starting with the librarian, the programme is gone through systematically as far as possible. Corpse dons his working attire – pair of PT shorts – and amid baths of sweat, gets cracking.

15.00 hours. Gasping Corpse, after using up calories at an alarming rate, rushes out armed with mug at the magic cry of 'shay-wallah' in the mid-distance. He is lucky enough for once to secure a pint of blessed tea before the NAAFI man is sold out.

16.30 hours. The Corpse, feverishly laying the slab floor of EPP House, is pierced to the marrow by the discordant shriek of the Orderly Sergeant's whistle, calling afternoon parade. Leaving hammer poised in mid-air, the Corpse sets up new record for 100 yards in reaching tent, donning overalls and falling in on parade before the Sergeant Major comes out.

18.30 hours. Threading his way painfully through the mob in the wash room, the Corpse finds a spare couple of inches on which to park his shaving mirror, and proceeds to clean himself up a bit. By the time he gets through he finds, as usual, that the last unsavoury remains of the evening meal are being cleared away. Customary ceremony with the oozing slime follows as before.

19.00 hours. To accompaniment of rosy tones of sunset, Corpse returns to 'Morgue' to find that lamp, as usual, is out of paraffin. Calls at Quartermaster's Stores for paraffin. Quartermaster's Stores is out of paraffin. Corpse returns to Morgue, shovels sand from afternoon sandstorm from bed and makes it up for the night. Job unnecessarily complicated through being done in dark, and causes much profanity. Thinking he might be able to snatch five minutes to read 'Palestine Post', Corpse makes off at high speed towards NAAFI. On picking up paper, notices it is a quarter of an hour past Library opening time and arranged-for librarian has not turned up. Angry crowd armed with volumes for exchange collects at booking desk. Corpse dashes off after Librarian, at whose tent he is informed said gentleman has gone to Jerusalem and nobody knows what he has done with the key. Changing course sharply for abode of Head Librarian (away on leave) Corpse obtains duplicate key and, eventually, after covering great distances of desert, arrives back at NAAFI in state of exhaustion. Opens Library and deals with greater part of hostile crowds; it then being 20 minutes after time 'Thursday Club' meeting should have commenced – tells remainder they have 'had it', and closes up again. On way over to Toc H tent, Corpse suddenly remembers he has not decided what to give Lecture on, leave alone do any preparation for same. Makes up mind and jots down a dozen main headings while Secretary is delivering Minutes of last meeting.

20.30. hours. Delivers entirely impromptu lecture, which is well received by scanty audience. Interesting discussion follows, as a result of which Corpse gets so 'het up' that he feels more awake at 23.30 hours when meeting finally breaks up, than he has done all day.

24.00 or 00.00 hours. Walks back to lines with E & WO. Sentries are slightly taken aback to hear animated discussion on future policy between the two, as they walk. Arrived back at Morgue, Corpse looks in usual place for urinal bucket. Bucket is not there. After circumnavigating camp three times and being challenged by about 34 sentries, eventually finds a bucket, and goes in to bed.

You might think this is the end of the story; but it is not. Corpse, mind far above mundane things, falls down steps in dark, and lands with crash on to bed of one 'Killer Lee' who, in the barbarous jargon in which the denizens of Oldham converse, enquires what the ?"!"&@£;: (etc etc.) Corpse apologies, and promptly falls over rubbish bin, kicking up tremendous clatter and waking whole tent. After this he is obliged to give an account of the evening's proceedings to make amends.

00.10 hours. The Corpse sinks back into his normal state of coma, and dreams of the happy days of long ago.

Curtain

The foregoing account was part of our attempt to counter boredom with humour, but, for me, it contained more than a germ of truth. This was that, though the unit was officially doing almost nothing, B Squadron Corpse was in fact obviously over-working. This was observed by one of our kinder and more perspicacious sergeants, one 'Chalky White', who very kindly arranged a 'holiday' for me.

Another sign of permanence was the establishment of a rest centre for NCOs of the hard pressed Middle East Forces. This was on the coast near to Gaza and was a very pleasant seaside site. The centre required a small number of 'other ranks' to act as waiters serving meals to the group of sergeants then at the centre. This, of course, was a typical Army 'non-job' involving almost no actual work for the waiters, and was really a holiday for them also.

So, thanks to the kindness of 'Chalky White' I was given a much needed break and chance to re-charge my batteries. So followed a strange episode in the life of B Squadron Corpse. From the totally communal atmosphere of The Morgue, your moribund friend was suddenly discharged into one of total inactivity and intense battery-recharging. All the staff had separate sleeping quarters, so apart from occasional meetings in the kitchen, there were no contacts at all. I spent my time catching up on arrears of my letters home, and in part lazing and taking in the peace and beauty of the seaside setting. I recall this as one of the happiest periods of my war service, partly on account of being freed, temporarily, of Army discipline.

One episode only, sticks in my mind from this peaceful period. There was a local tradition of placing nets on the cliff tops to catch quails flying in at cliff top level. I have an idea that this practice dates back to Old Testament days. The cook, who evidently took pride in providing meals very much better than Army fare, had planned a treat for his sergeants, by following the old custom and setting up his own nets on the cliff tops. These netted an adequate meal's worth of the unfortunate quails, which are very tiny birds and seemingly unsuitable for food.

So thought a most unlikely conservationist in the shape of a kitchen assistant, originally from the Glasgow slums, known just as 'Jock'. Jock felt strongly enough about it to start a free fight in the kitchen in an attempt to rescue the quails. Unfortunately, like so many conservationists, he found himself outgunned, and the sergeants did get their special dinner, which I had to carry in. The cooked quails, so minute, looked particularly pathetic and I found myself totally in sympathy with Jock.

Again, I was reminded that every Garden of Eden has its serpent; even this quiet backwater on the Palestine coast. How odd that today, in the 1990s, the position should be precisely reversed. In 1942 the whole world was at war but the then British-administered Palestine was a haven of peace. Today, the Gaza strip is one of the several areas where murderous racial conflicts disgrace modern civilisation.

For me, my holiday duly came to an end, and only the periodic official 'leaves' punctuated the boredom of Rafah. But how fortunate I was to be able to take these in an area so packed with history as the Holy Land. Ancient Jerusalem and ultra-modern Tel Aviv were the principal leave centres, with the smaller port of Haifa as an alternative. For me, by special dispensation of the Squadron authorities, there was also one magical leave in Lebanon, and by my own ingenuity, in adding a wireless telegraphy course in Cairo on to another leave, to see that, then, marvellous old city and to take a trip as far as Luxor on the Nile. For me, these opportunities of seeing so much of historical interest at the expense of HM Government more than compensated for all the boredom and discomfort inflicted on me.

1. Matilda tanks in battle array. If General Lord Gort had had even 100 more of these in 1940 for his one, failed counter offensive, he might have halted the German offensive in France, there might have been no Dunkirk, and the course of the war might have altered.

2. *A Matilda tank with standard 2-pounder gun.*

3. *Matilda tank with CDL turret, showing on the left the vertical slot where the light beam emerged and on the right the Besa machine gun which was its only conventional weapon. Our text records how the 11th Bn. Royal Tank Regt. spent much of its time changing between gun and CDL turrets.*

4. C Squadron Buffaloes parked before loading troops of the 52nd Lowland Division for the attack on South Beveland.

5. Just after typhoons had attacked. Headquarters ship pulling out to allow LCT to beach.

6. In the perilous 'gap' at Westkapelle, shortly after the first landing. A Buffalo is just landing a group of Royal Marine Commandos.

7. One of 79th Armoured Division's special vehicles, a 'Crab' adaptation of a Sherman tank, landing in the 'gap'. Chains attached to its rotating drum beat the ground, exploding any mines that might lie in its path.

8. Near Antwerp, October 1944. Monty inspects a V2.

9. Sir Winston Churchill speaking to men of 11 Royal Tanks; beside him Field Marshal Montgomery. The picture shows also several faces I recognise but can no longer name. However, prominent to the left of the group is my old friend and colleague who accompanied me through his war service, Trooper Leslie Myers (with coat turned back), and to the far right Trooper (Killer) Lee, both of whom appear in the text.

10. *If any one man could be credited with winning the war, it was surely Churchill. Here, he is mounted in a Sherman Tank and smoking one of the cigars which became his trademark.*

11. *Churchill ceremonially crossing the Rhine (see caption of following picture). To his right is Trooper Cooper, a well remembered colleague of the author. Before the war, Cooper was a racecourse bookmaker.*

Lt.-Col. S. F. T. B. Lever. G.S.O.1 (Ops) 79. Armoured Division.

Field Marshal Sir Alan Brooke C.T, G.S.

Lt.-Col. S. I. Howard-Jones. O.C. IIth ROYAL TANKS.

Lt.-Gen. Sir Miles Dempsey. Commander Second Army.

The Prime Minister.

Lt.-Gen. M. M. Ritchie Commander 12 Corps.

G. O. C.

The C. in C.

12. *The Prime Minister, accompanied by senior officers, making a ceremonial crossing of the Rhine in a Buffalo of B Squadron 11th RTR, after the military operation had been successfully completed. The author's old colleague, Sergeant Goodman, is in command of the craft.*

By the autumn of 1942 our leave quota was in full swing, but until then we had to cope with what Rafah had to offer: mainly sand. Perhaps this is the moment for a brief essay on sand, analogous to the one on mud at Penrith. At Rafah you lived among sand, you slept among it: it got into your blankets, kitbags, socks, toothpaste, boot polish, underclothes and watch; more intimately, in your eyes, ears, nose, throat and hair, and your food always contained liberal quantities. In short, it was impossible to find a place, indoors or out, where sand was not. Of course, it was soft and usually dry and, unlike mud, would shake out reasonably easily. When it was in a static condition we became used to it, and resigned. It was when it started blowing about in the form of sand storms that it became really virulent and this it did every time when the surface was dry. A real sandstorm, of which we had quite a few, is just about the most objectionable natural phenomenon I have experienced. You are smothered, stifled, suffocated: about the only way you would really keep it out would be to wear a gas mask. It would, moreover, hang around for some time before and after the actual storm, seeming to circle round you in cyclonic fashion. During the whole time the sky turned a dirty greyish brown and the air thick and choking. With the approach of winter the sandstorms became less frequent, to everyone's relief. On the voyage out to the Middle East, our boys became very fed up with the sight of endless sea: many would become glad to have back the water, in place of the equally monotonous desert.

Actually, Palestine consisted mainly of only semi-desert: proof of its potential fertility lay in the way in which cultivated areas were reclaimed from the desert by the industrious Jewish community, in spite of scarcity of natural vegetation such that individual trees were shown on the map as landmarks. In time, this has led to the establishment of the huge Israeli citrus fruit industry: perhaps today the finest in the world.

The procedure was, first, to surround the area with a prickly pear hedge, giving some protection from the blowing sand, then planting it sparsely with ordinary shrubs such as we plant in our gardens. Then the permanent crop, such as maize, olives or oranges would appear. Sometimes also grapes, leading to a substantial local wine industry. The landscape is usually broken up by groups of cypresses. Cupressus Macrocarpa, which I tried in vain to grow in England, did particularly well.

But in the southern, non-mountainous, part of the country the orange and lemon groves covered the greatest area and set up patterns for the landscape, planted close together in serried rows, giving solid patches of deep, emerald green. The individual orange tree is not a bit romantic-looking and in no way to be compared with, say, the lordly date palm. It is a small bush, something between privet and laurel in appearance, but thickly covered in shiny green leaves. From a distance, the whole area looked solid green, interspersed with patches of orange, for there appeared to be no definite flowering or fruiting season. Individual trees could be seen carrying blossom, green fruit and ripe fruit at the same time.

But not less marvellous than the greenery of the desert were the Jewish communal settlements that followed, sometimes hastily and perhaps shoddily built, but a true triumph of the human spirit against natural adversity. From observation on the spot then, I find myself today, in the present conflict, strongly pro-Israeli and anti-Arab. Having been in undisputed possession of the land for 2,000 years the Arabs did absolutely nothing to improve it, while the Israelis, in an incredibly short time, have turned much of it back into the Biblical land flowing with milk and honey.

A particular case was that of the city of Tel Aviv, which when I knew it during the War, was then brand new. Taking the patch of barren desert adjoining the ancient port of Jaffa, the Jewish settlers in a period of only 20 years had built a completely new city of, then, some 250,000 inhabitants, mostly refugees from a Europe which had rejected them. Most of them were of German origin, speaking Yiddish, but there was also a substantial Russian minority, escapees from the then Soviet system. At that time, it was also an intellectual city with a high proportion of academics, once leaders of European society. To see a one-time professor selling matches on a street corner was not uncommon.

One restaurant, introduced to me by the hedonistic and well educated Corporal Livsey, who was then expecting to be given a commission, offered truly superb food and hospitality such as might be expected by a favoured customer back in Germany. The proprietor went by the title of 'Herr Doctor'. So in Tel Aviv we were back to the flesh pots. I have often wondered what subsequently happened to Livsey, who was one of those who had a natural capacity for getting into trouble which seemed constantly to be thwarting the progress of his military career. It was at his suggestion that we tried a swim in the local River Yarkon, from which we were lucky to come out unscathed, for it turned out that we could have contracted the dreaded disease, bilharzia, from its infected waters.

But Tel Aviv offered food for the mind, as well as the stomach, for I remember attending an opera there. It was in Hebrew, but great music surmounts the barriers of language and the cheerful humour of *Die Fledermaus* was the ideal antidote to Army 'browned offness'. I later had the opportunity of seeing this masterpiece performed in its natural home, but I doubt if I ever enjoyed it more than in its Hebrew presentation at Tel Aviv.

No doubt much has changed since I saw Tel Aviv in 1942, but then, while not belittling this triumph of man over nature, I found the city would not stand up to too close an inspection. Already, some of the dazzling white houses were getting dirty and the odd unfinished corner spoiled the general effect: rather like a slatternly woman, beautifully made-up, but whose make-up was beginning to wear off. Contrary to general opinion in the Squadron, I found I preferred the solid construction and beautiful architecture of Jerusalem.

I was privileged, I believe, in having a leave to coincide with Christmas 1942, and in being able to spend this in Jerusalem, surely the ultimate repository of history combined with religious sentiment. After seeing Jerusalem in its golden glory, one re-reads the Bible with renewed interest. The ancient city stands on a series of hills, giving it a pleasantly broken outline, and is built entirely of the local stone, varying between cream and reddish in colour. Under the mid-day sun it glows warmly: in the bright moonlight it is shimmering white. One could indeed imagine it to be the gate to heaven.

The best viewpoint is from the Mount of Olives, 2,650 feet above sea level. In the foreground is the Valley of Kedron, then beyond is the Old City surrounded by its wall, clustered on a hill top with its towers, minarets and churches, the whole giving an impression of fortress-like solidity. The huge lead dome of the Mosque of Omar dominates this viewpoint.

Behind, in the New City, a palatial effect was crowned by a huge campanile which was, at that time, not the Parliament building, but the YMCA, reflecting that, then, the important institution in Jerusalem was the British Middle East Army. I wonder what function it performs today?

Jerusalem, I found, is one of the few ancient cities where the modern part did not spoil the old: rather it enhanced it. Architectural styles varied between Moorish, Byzantine and modern American, yet no single feature seemed discordant. Perhaps the main reason was the uniformity of the building material, combined with sundry outcrops of natural rock.

Everywhere, there was variation of level with frequent flights of steps between streets, little courts with eucalyptus trees and patches of purple bougainvillea, even small burial grounds. An apparently solid mass of masonry, examined in more detail, recorded the remains of three older cities, one below the other, and each containing something historically significant. If ever, and Heaven forbid, the present Israeli-Arab racial hatred should break into open warfare over ownership of Jerusalem, I imagine the ancient city would stand up well to modern artillery.

One could see so many New Testament sites: the Citadel, known as the Tower of David; the Pool of Bethesda, the Via Dolorosa, the route of the Cross; the site of the Temple, now occupied by the Mosque of Omar; the house of Caiphas, the High Priest; the Holy Sepulchre, the supposed site of Calvary.

One hopes that this has since been rectified, but the Holy Sepulchre, supposedly the most sacred of Christian sites, was made ridiculous by the various sects being unable to agree upon which of them should guard the key to the building. Eventually they handed it to a Moslem to hold. Similarly, a small piece of carpet surrounding the altar was actually divided into segments: one for Roman Catholics, once for Greek Orthodox, one for Armenians, one for Copts, etc. This, after the crusades to recover the Holy Places from the Moslems.

I was not impressed by the Holy Sepulchre. One could buy for 50 piastres (about 5p) a certificate stating that one had visited the Holy Places – indeed it was difficult to avoid doing so. The whole thing was too reminiscent of the money changers in the Temple.

I much preferred the, then, rival site for the location of Calvary, known as 'Gordon's Calvary', the celebrated hero of Khartoum having been a strong advocate of this theory. This is sited outside the Damascus Gate, and thus outside the City Wall, as the hymn states, and also is overlooked by a remarkable rock formation closely resembling a human skull, 'Golgotha, the place of the skull' described in the scriptures.

A similar controversy arose over the celebrated Wailing Wall of the Jews. They maintain that this was one of the original walls of Solomon's Temple. According to the Moslems, however, it dates only from the Temple built by Herod the Great. Whoever is right, it is still very, very ancient. The Wailing Wall marks the boundary on the city side of the ornate Mosque of Omar, with its outer walls in patterned blue tiles and interior completely covered in elaborate mosaic, the base for which is alleged to be gold.

One of the most powerfully atmospheric sites I found to be the Garden of Gethsemane which still contains what are said to be some of the original olive trees there in the time of Christ. That any living organism could have survived so long in time and through so much strife certainly gives pause for thought.

Bethlehem, to one's surprise, turned out to be only a mile or so out of Jerusalem. There was a bus but one could walk it easily. Whether this would still be so today is doubtful, but in 1942 I found Bethlehem the loveliest little white town, perched steeply on a hillside at the edge of the cultivated terraces surrounding the city of Jerusalem. In a campanile above the Church of the Nativity are the bells of Bethlehem which are still broadcast at Christmas. Bethlehem came about as near to converting an unbeliever as any symbol can get.

The tiny doorway, reduced three times in size for purpose of defence, makes it necessary to 'duck' to enter, reminding one of the pronouncement 'it is easier for a camel to pass through the eye of a needle than for a rich man to enter into the Kingdom of Heaven'. If one did not know that this was a church, it would be taken for the fortress it has in fact also been.

From Jerusalem, I did a general tour of the Holy Land, and the main surprise was what a tiny country this is. One can cover all the main centres of interest in a single day, for I did just that in a 250-mile car journey. It took me right round the Sea of Galilee as far as Capernaum, and back partly through Jordan. We were back in Jerusalem by 5.00 pm. We passed through Nablus (the ancient Schechem), Nazareth, Tiberias on the Sea of Galilee, the Valleys of Jezreel and Bashan-Og. The King of Bashan had stuck in my mind from childhood Bible stories, but I never realised what a fertile kingdom he had.

The Valley of Jezreel is said to be one of the most fertile spots on earth, with an estimated 40 feet depth of top soil – truly the land flowing with milk and honey; while in total contrast only some 40 miles away across the Jordan are the desolate lands of Gilead and Moab.

In this single day I saw them all: Jacob's Well where he wrestled with the angel; the place where Abraham attempted to sacrifice his son, Isaac; the hill down which the swine rushed into the waters of the Sea of Galilee; the battlefield where King Saul was slain by the Philistines; Cana of Galilee, scene of the miracle of the loaves and fishes; the cave where the Holy Family lived and Joseph carried on his carpentry. Even the names were largely unchanged since Biblical times. About the closest packed day of vivid impressions of my whole long life.

Translating to the present day, one cannot help but notice that the fertile regions – bearing in mind that in the south of the country the Jewish settlers created them out of barren desert – are all in Israeli hands while the bare, rocky hills of the West Bank, the Biblical Samaria, are Arab territory, where the latter are bitterly resisting further encroachments by the Jewish settlers. One wonders whether the Jewish settlers, if given their head, might not succeed in turning the rocky wilderness, somewhat resembling the Eastern Highlands of Scotland, into as fertile and productive an area as they have made the southern desert. Jacob and Ishmael are still with us today.

One area not covered by my tour was the port of Haifa, which became the site of another leave. It was small as ports go, but then of great importance as the terminal of the Iraq-Iran oil pipeline; and probably more so today as the port for export of the products of the Israeli fruit industry.

Jerusalem was the ultimate historical and religious monument; Tel Aviv was a miracle of modern city construction out of nothing; but Haifa, back in 1942, was the place for the English to live. And, it must be remembered that back in those days of the Second World War, what was then Palestine was still a British protectorate and very much under British rule. The administrators and government officials had to live somewhere, and where they chose to live was Haifa.

Haifa bears some resemblance, on a miniature scale, to another strange left-over from the British Empire, Hong Kong, which has lasted, strangely, right up to the present day. It lies on the tip of a tongue of land projecting into the Mediterranean, of which the backbone is the mini-mountain of Mount Carmel. Exactly as I knew from my childhood used to happen in Hong Kong with the local Chinese, the undistinguished Arab town lay at the foot of the hill round the harbour, the Jewish communities half way up, but the

British, of course, lived on top. Neat gardens fronted dwellings with such names as 'Mon Repos' and a notice on the gate bearing the standard legend 'No Hawkers – Beware of the Dog' which they did not even bother to translate into Arabic. A breath of Old England in a foreign land, if ever there was one.

Again, my hotel in Haifa catered for Britons and whereas in Tel Aviv the diet was mainly Continental, in Haifa roast beef and two veg predominated.

Haifa also supported a flourishing night life and, after dark, coloured lights announced the identity of numerous night clubs. There were German-type beer gardens, fronting a tree-lined avenue leading up from the sea to the elaborate Casino. Bands played Strauss waltzes while couples danced silently on small dance floors set among the trees, now disappearing like ghosts into the shadows, now standing out hard in the starlight. Soft lapping of Mediterranean waves made a background to the music and night creatures whispered in the trees. It was all very beautiful, and such a contrast to our own patch of desert at Rafah.

Some of the more international-style night clubs even contained a, by now, almost forgotten sight – beautiful women and attempts to emulate on a tiny scale the magnificent dance ensembles of the 1930s American film choreographer, Busby Berkeley.

The Jewish-run clubs tended to produce a more earthy style of entertainment. One night I made the mistake of taking up an offer of taxi transport to the night club area and joining a party destined for a certain Jewish club. I have to say this with regret, but the Jewish community of that time did not produce beautiful women. They tended to be short and fat with the head jammed directly on to the shoulders without any detectable neck joining them. This club was liberally staffed with hostesses, all expecting to be bought drinks. One such attached herself to my group and reciprocated with an endless repertoire of dirty stories: 'want to hear another one?' It was not my scene and this, to me, was a wasted evening. But the birds still sang on Mount Carmel and on one occasion, exploring its craggy summit, I disturbed a large bird of prey, which might possibly have been an eagle, from its nest. It flew away, screaming, so I was not reduced to defending myself with my 'jack knife'.

From the summit, with its scent of flowers and pine needles, one could see occasional Arab shepherds with their flocks, and also some cattle, with Swiss-style bells around their necks, and distant views across the Valley of Jezreel with the snow covered mountains of Lebanon in the distance, capped by the 11,000 foot cone of Mount Hermon. I was sorry indeed to leave Haifa.

Occasionally, in addition to the leaves, we benefited from the occasional spell of 'special training', which was, in effect, another free holiday. One day we had a round trip by lorry to Jericho and the Dead Sea. This happened during the next Spring, a season when the desert again bloomed. As this was an official trip we went by lorry, making possible a more interesting route which a hired car could not have managed. We crossed the central mountain chain of Palestine, with its high moorland areas somewhat resembling the eastern Highlands of Scotland, scarred by deep gullies and ravines and with drops of 1,000 feet or more abutting the track.

At this time of the year, though it would shortly return to the barren norm, sufficient grass was showing to cover the hills green instead of brown and there was a wealth of flowers which would not shame the fertile valleys of the Alps. But, as one descended one entered again the abomination of desolation of the Dead Sea area, the area where once were the cities of Sodom and Gomorrah which Jehovah destroyed and sowed the site with salt. As always, he made a pretty good job of it. The salt content of the Dead Sea is many times that of normal seawater and it is impossible to swim in it as the water is so dense that a body cannot submerge.

Down and down we went to the lowest spot of any land on earth, some 1,300 feet below the Mediterranean sea level, experiencing a change of climate en route, for the valley bottom was as hot as hell with nothing in sight but bare rock and salt, and salt and salt. One could see the pillar of salt into which Lot's wife is recorded to have been changed.

Further south is the Red Sea and the spot where the Israelites were supposed to have crossed by Jehovah dividing the waters, creating a bridge of dry land for them to escape the pursuing Egyptian chariots, dropping the sea back to normal when they had crossed and drowning the unfortunate Egyptians.

Here, there is a factual postscript of some interest, for the Pharaoh pursuing them has been identified, his body recovered and buried in the traditional Egyptian manner in the Valley of the Kings. But, for him, the usual process of mummification was not necessary, for he, too, had been converted into a solid body of salt, giving apparent confirmation of the Biblical story of the crossing of the Red Sea.

This was not the first apparent confirmation in my own experience of an improbable classical story. When I visited the site of ancient Troy, now in western Turkey, I was surprised to note how tiny this most ancient city was. The story is that, after their duel, the victorious Achilles dragged the body of the defeated Trojan, Hector, round the walls of the city, attached to his chariot. I saw for myself that the apparently impossible feat was perfectly feasible .

Another point of interest worth noting is the colossal error by the early archaeologist, Schliemann, who in his excavation of Troy cleared away masses of rubble, assuming that the Troy of Greek legend had to be the lowest level of building revealed. But he was very, very wrong for modern archaeologists have discovered that there were no fewer than nine older cities buried beneath the present upper ruins. What Schliemann had done was to shovel away the remains of the city he was trying to uncover.

But to return to the lowest spot on earth and the confluence of the River Jordan with the Dead Sea. This is the site of the still existing city of Jericho. Jericho, unfortunately, no longer showed any firm evidence of the collapse of the city wall in response to the blare of trumpets of Joshua's Israelite Army. But it is situated in a green and verdant haven, showing that even in the most blasted of salty deserts an oasis can exist.

6
Beyond the Holy Land

After this visit to the lowest spot on earth, my next leave was to one of the Middle East's highest spots, the subsequently ill-fated country of Lebanon.

The most imaginative of the many charitable organisations catering for the welfare of British troops in the area was the Church of Scotland and it was to my friend the Squadron Welfare Officer's contact with them that I owed this colossal favour. It was rumoured that a new leave centre had been established at the well named Dhour-El-Choir (haven of peace) under Church of Scotland auspices, near to Beirut. This was obviously the sort of place for the further recovery from desert ennui of B Squadron Corpse, and I, alone of the Squadron, took up the offer with enthusiasm.

Lebanon is even smaller than Palestine, there being only 50 miles between the Mediterranean coast and the Syrian border. But in this tiny space there are two parallel major mountain ranges, the Lebanon and the Anti-Lebanon, separated by the broad Bekaa Valley, which contains, to my mind, in Baalbek, one of the finest of all classical Greek ruined temple sites.

Behind Beirut in the Lebanon range was Djebel Sunnein, at 8,500 feet, the area to which I was bound, while further north, behind Tripoli, was a peak of over 10,000 feet. The Anti-Lebanon range, overlooking Damascus, said to be the world's oldest still inhabited city, culminated in the magnificent dome of Mount Hermon, permanently snow covered at nearly 11,000 feet. A more complete contrast to our below sea level desert could hardly be imagined.

Again, in this tiny area, there was an incredible variation of climate. In contrast to the fresh and pleasant mountain areas, Beirut, in August 1943, was as hot as hell. The narrow coastal strip between mountains and sea is very humid and a cloud of damp heat haze hangs over the city. A glance at the street thermometer showed over 100 degrees F and this, in a damp heat, was unbearably hot even for me, who likes heat.

Nevertheless, Beirut in 1943 was a very beautiful city, making what has happened to it since then all the more tragic. At this time it was part of the then vast French colonial empire, never quite as large as the British, but comprising the whole of North Africa and substantial parts of the Middle East. The British and French always had diametrically opposed colonial policies. The British approach was always to govern through the existing native institutions; to the French their empire was 'La France outre Mer', incidentally the name of a prominent Paris museum. A French lady with whom I once took tea described it as France is not so much a country, as a way of life. So it was in Beirut back in 1943 as part of the huge areas coloured green on the map; almost as impressive as the even vaster areas coloured red.

The French city of 1943 was beautifully laid out, very much in the traditional French style, with well proportioned squares, colonnades and fountains, and wrought iron fronted balconies. But, as with all the new French cities – it was exactly the same in Morocco – there was an absolute division between the French city and the native. Not that the latter was in its way at all inferior. Beirut, in 1943, provided the most perfect examples of the archetypal oriental bazaar such as existed in the time of the Sultan, Harun el Rashid. There were streets of shoemakers, jewellers, leather workers, metal workers – even shirt makers: all the trades of the traditional East.

However, fascinating as Beirut was in 1943, one could hardly remain there long in that heat, and in any case one's time on leave was limited. Reluctant as I was to leave the French-style pavement cafés, where coffee, cognac and the potent local spirit, arak, were consumed in an atmosphere of gaiety, so different from that of the restrained German type cafes of Tel Aviv, I was propelled upwards to cooler climes, even allowing for the French culture of Beirut having provided at least one cool place in the shape of air conditioned cinemas.

So, I found myself a ramshackle bus bound for Dhour-el-Choir and we, that is a motley selection of local inhabitants, with their attendant smells, duly packed into a vehicle far too small to contain all of us, the smells, and oxygen as well. Before embarking, there was much juggling with a local currency consisting wholly of paper money, varying from a magnificent note of many colours for one livre (pound) but worth only about ten pence in our today's money, ranging down to small change which appeared to consist of old bus tickets stuck together with stamp edging.

Our ancient bus – it was a tribute to early motor engineering that it could make it – climbed steadily for some two hours into purer air. We passed through villages in a lush countryside growing bananas, dates, pomegranates, etc, passing the last of the city's trams with humanity hanging from their sides like bunches of grapes. The villages exuded prosperity, in marked contrast to the miserable mud huts of the Arab area of Palestine. Nearly all the houses seemed to be new and built of local stone, though in the Arabic style, the red tile roofs blending with the colouring of the landscape. Fruit was for sale in abundance everywhere at give-away prices, but it was hardly necessary to buy it, for the stuff practically fell on one's head in passing.

This was a Christian region of Lebanon and here I must confess to being wholly on the side of the Christians in the destructive civil wars which have rent this paradise of a country in the intervening years. Arabs, once they have adopted it, seem to take their Christianity pretty seriously and, to me, most of the aggressive characteristics of the race seem to be associated with the Moslem religion.

Arrived at Dhour-el-Choir, I made enquiries for St Andrew's Hostel. Having been directed practically everywhere within a 30 mile radius, I eventually found it by ignoring the local instructions ('Yes George, me know St Andrews, you come this way, me very good, quick, etc') and using my own judgement. At 4,500 feet above sea level, this was a different world.

The hostel turned out to be a former school, stone-built in the monastic style, with stone flagged floors, timbered roof and arched alcoves. The dining hall, in particular, with wooden minstrels' gallery and timbered ceiling looked positively medieval. Its appointments, to one used to Army style living, were excellent, though of course in this remote spot one did not expect, and did not get, running water. A stone pitcher, of the kind women carry on their heads in the East, contained sweet, ice-cold mountain water.

The Hotel was run by an American couple, helped out by sundry missionaries on holiday. Considering that the place was used almost exclusively for British troops, it was a generous gesture on the part of the Americans.

On entering the dining hall, I was amazed and embarrassed to find that we were waited upon by little girls, aged from about seven to fourteen. Some were the daughters of the missionaries and some local Lebanese schoolgirls, some of apparently Greek or Armenian race, but speaking Arabic. I was particularly taken by one, very junior girl, a perfect example of Arab femininity. Her name was Julie, and her job was to fill the glasses of water. It seemed queer to see this dusky child working alongside the blue-eyed, flaxen haired and demure little American girls.

There was one ten-year-old boy whose job was serving mid-morning lemonade, who made my own travel record look very silly. He had been to Britain, Canada, USA, Egypt, Jordan, Palestine, Syria, Iraq, Iran, India, Burma and most of the European countries. Missionaries certainly have unique opportunities to travel and in Lebanon in 1943 they had fertile ground for their main activity.

On a Sunday evening a service was held at the hostel and an Arab boy who worked about the place asked me why I had not attended. Was I not a Christian? I was hard put to know how to reply for it was clear that a candid 'no' would have shocked him terribly. I tried to tell him that I had attended service regularly while I was at school, omitting to add that it was compulsory there, but opportunities in the Army were limited. Again, untrue, for there were compulsory and unpopular Church parades.

Another discovery I made was how politically conscious the Lebanese were. I had always thought that the Free French movement, while France was under Nazi control, was supported by the British largely for their own purposes, but Beirut and neighbourhood were plastered with portraits of General de Gaulle. Yet, though French culture was so omnipresent, the French administration was clearly not popular and, of course, ended promptly with the end of the War: hardly surprisingly, for French colonialists struck me as even more arrogant than the British. While I was in Lebanon a Frenchman spoke to me only once, and that was to ask for a match.

The locals, by contrast, could not have been more welcoming. In Egypt and Palestine, British soldiers were accepted on sufferance solely on account of what 'backshesh' could be extracted from them. In Dhour-el-Choir we were accepted for our own sakes. Not only was I not pestered for 'backshesh' but had endless offers of fruit from local peasants, who refused to take money in exchange. I had several offers to come in for a meal and, on one occasion, I accepted, and a very good meal it was, too, and a beautifully clean house. Taking my French nice and slowly, I also had an interesting conversation.

Here we have perhaps the answer to the contradictions of today's Arab nationalism, and why the various peoples will probably never unite. How can people whose main object in life is to extract 'backshesh' unite with those who do not accept it?

But back to the mountains – which I was why I had mainly come to Dhour-el-Choir. Following the apparently logical policy of pursuing main excursions while one is fresh, I determined to tackle Mt Sunnein the next day. As a practised mountaineer I should have known better, for I was ignoring that I had come from Rafah, which was slightly below sea level, and to attempt to climb straight to 8,500 feet without a period of acclimatisation was against all the established principles of the craft. Not surprisingly, the result was that a mountain defeated me for the first time, and the last until, at age then of almost 79, I found I could not climb higher in the Himalayas than about 17,000 feet.

I was told that the climb could just about be managed in the day, but the good people at the hostel were horrified that I should be attempting this alone. So, out of consideration for their feelings, I found myself a companion for the climb. He turned out to be that supposed arch enemy of all soldiers, a military policeman, but in fact was a very decent man and I enjoyed his company – which proves, I suppose, that one should never condemn any kind of grouping out of hand.

Armed with enormous quantities of food we set off along the ridge on which our village was placed, which led on to the main ridge leading to the summit, passing through a picturesque village with the name 'Bois de Boulogne'. Parisian influence certainly penetrated. After a 7.00 am start, 11.30 am found us only at the saddle giving on to the main ridge and, at around 7,000 feet, the effect of rarefied atmosphere was making itself felt, whereas in the Alps I had climbed considerably higher without feeling any effect at all.

From whatever cause, however, my companion 'conked out' at this stage, being badly sick, so I left him with half the rations and sent him down at his leisure, later finding out that he had duly recovered. This showed that my original judgement was correct: that it was safer for an experienced mountaineer to climb alone rather than with an untried novice, although he was young and fit. I could easily have been left with a sick man on my hands on a deserted mountain, hours from any help. It was partly from young, untried novices being included in the party that the fatal disaster occurred on the first ascent of the Matterhorn.

However, the last 500 feet were steeper and to my amazement and chagrin I, also, felt the full effect of altitude for the first time. My legs turned to lead and I had no energy to drag them further. Also a feeling of extreme depression settled on me. What was the point? Why was I subjecting myself to such discomfort? Altitude apparently acts something like alcohol: up to a point it stimulates; after that it knocks you out.

So, partly in view of the time and the increasing slowness of my progress – it is always easy to find good reasons for abandoning a difficult project – I turned back, strength returning with every downward step. I had, for the first time, to admit that a mountain had beaten me.

Another thing I had not taken into account was inadequacy of Army boots for climbing and how soft my feet had become after a year on sand. By the time I was down to the hostel they were not just blistered, but bruised to the point of making walking an agony.

The next day, from necessity, I took rather easily, doing nothing but looking round the small local cigarette factory. It was an anomaly that with the huge tobacco enterprises there were in England I should have come to this remote spot to see cigarettes manufactured for the first time.

Also, I eased my sore feet by patronising the local swimming pool. An ancient Arab made a living charging 25 piastres a time for its use. What a pleasure was this pool, only 30 feet long, but probably as deep, and fed by an ice-cold mountain stream. A bathe in this, after the luke-warm and sticky sea was a delight indeed.

I also spent an interesting, if unprofitable, evening trying to persuade the local shoemaker to put some studs on the soles of my boots. Having finally, by tri-lingual conversation reinforced by gestures, got the point home as to what I wanted, the transaction ended on the point that it was Sunday, so he could not do the job, anyway. I had overlooked that this was a Christian village where they take their Christianity seriously.

On my next day I met another laddie, stationed locally, who knew something of these parts and wanted to try Sunnein. He conceived the idea of trying it at night by moonlight. I was delighted to find a man even madder than myself, so, of course, I fell for this idea. In any case, I was obliged to revenge my previous defeat, so the trip was arranged for after dinner the same night. The setting sun saw us stepping out manfully while the missionaries offered up prayers for our safety and, I feel sure, must have started organising a search party as soon as we had gone.

Taking a different route this time, we descended first to the bottom of our own valley some 1,000 or 1,500 feet, following a road at right angles to Sunnein's escarpment, leaving about 6,000 feet actually to climb. We passed jauntily through a couple of villages accompanied by amazed stares of the local inhabitants who surely thought we were mad. And who should say that they were wrong? An hour and a half's going saw us across the floor of the gorge, eerily walled in by echoing rocks and peaks just visible in the sunset's afterglow.

The Middle East is at its best at sunset, with the failing light bringing out the colours: the predominantly reddish rocks with purple splashes indicating rich mineral deposit. For colour, these mountains equalled any, even the glorious Alps. Around 11.00 pm we passed our last village and the moon rose over Sunnein's crest, bathing the valley in ghostly iridescence, with twinkling lights marking the villages we had passed. We found it amply light for climbing for the rest of the night, even for the final scramble up the steep escarpment, mostly consisting of loose scree. It was one of those stepped escarpments of which you do not see the full extent from below. It appeared to be a straight slope, but did not reveal the 'flats' in between.

It was 4.00 am before, after some crawling on hands and knees, we reached the summit ridge only to find that what had appeared to be a straightforward summit was in fact a huge plateau, probably a couple of miles across, and consisting of rock and scree. This plateau was covered with countless craters, clearly of volcanic origin, interspersed with hills, any one of which might have been the official summit.

After wandering about this plateau for about an hour, falling into snow-filled craters, we sat down for breakfast and waited for dawn, which came about 5.30 am. The dawn revealed better this amazing landscape. In the light of subsequent landings on the moon, I would say that it closely resembled the surface of the latter.

Finally discovering the hut marking the true summit, we rewarded ourselves for our night's labour with the most magnificent view. To the west one could see the island of Cyprus; to the north the still higher summits behind Tripoli. To the east lay the broad Bekaa valley, neatly cut up into rectangles of cultivation, and dominated in the centre by the columns of Baalbek's ruined temples, clearly silhouetted in the rising sun. Beyond, again the Anti-Lebanon range dominated by Mount Hermon. To the south west were the foothills running down to Beirut and the coast, which one could see as far as Haifa over 100 miles away.

I had hoped while in Lebanon to see Baalbek, and perhaps even Damascus in Syria, but time did not permit in the ten days of my leave. In any case, I was reluctant to leave the home comforts of St Andrew's Hostel. So the final days passed in enjoying some of the glories of Lebanon, like its wonderful pure bred Arab horses, to my mind just about equine perfection. Beirut was a main centre for breeding. Almost any farmhouse had them being used for threshing or some such operation. For transportation, the mule was more often used as being more suited to mountain country than the horse or the ubiquitous donkey. They carried loads in civilised fashion in panniers strapped to their sides. None of the 'mobile haystack' syndrome so common in Palestine.

But Lebanon's crowning glory was surely its women. I imagine, as in Eastern countries, they are liable to fade early, but among young women I do not think during my long life since then that I have ever seen such a high standard of good looks. It was not so much that there were an unusual number of ravishing beauties, but simply that almost every woman one saw was good to look upon. One of my friends in the Squadron was, I fear, hurt by my suggestion that they put English girls completely in the shade, but such was my honest opinion.

To return from these dizzy heights to our favourite desert was indeed coming down to earth with a vengeance.

I had always hoped to see Lebanon again and indeed I did, although I had to wait until 1972 for this, by which time everything had so changed as to be unrecognisable. This was a classic example of the general principle that, generally, it is unwise to try to repeat a perfect experience. The occasion was a holiday in Cyprus, then, before the Turkish invasion which finally split the island, a delight in itself. From Cyprus, Beirut was only 20 minutes flight away and it seemed silly not to take advantage of being so near.

But before the aircraft had even landed I knew that it was a mistake. Coming in to land, instead of the graceful outlines of the French city, what greeted one was a mini New York of featureless tower blocks, looking quite like any other skyscraper city. Every trace of the formerly pervading French influence had disappeared, to be replaced by the universal American. So when the city was subsequently destroyed in the vicious civil war, in my eyes the damage that mattered had already been done. Not only the elegant balconies and colonnades had disappeared but also all the fascinating Eastern bazaar district.

That is not to say I did not enjoy at all my 48-hour visit. I did manage to see the other coastal cities, including Byblos, reputedly the oldest town on earth, and the incomparable Greek temples of Baalbek. I also saw a most sophisticated American floor show at the casino, which would have done credit to the 1930s' film dance spectacles of Busby Berkeley. But, however desirable, a mini Hollywood was not what one had come to see. Of course, all the showgirls were American. How much of this second, American style, Beirut survived the civil war or has since been replaced, I should need yet another visit to discover.

The biggest disappointment, however, was my nostalgic trip back to Dhour-el-Choir. It still existed, but absolutely nothing remained that I recognised, Mt Sunnein looked completely different and, of course, St Andrew's Hostel had disappeared. I could not even recognise where it had stood. I should have stayed away.

I had one more leave before the progress of the War left us behind, as usual. Rommel, bereft of reinforcements now that the Allied Air Forces again controlled the Mediterranean, had been expelled from North Africa, and the Middle East campaign and everything that went with it was virtually over. Came 1944 and the 11th Battalion RTR was at last moved back to Europe where it performed its only useful service.

But before this happened, I managed, by the usual devious devices, a leave in Cairo and a trip up the Nile. This will be dealt with in a separate later chapter. What happened was that, by again manipulating the help of my various friends in the Squadron, I made use of my official designation as a wireless operator to ask for a refresher course in Morse signalling, then held in Cairo. This was so timed that it could be tacked on to my real leave, leaving a holiday long enough for some Egyptian exploration.

That the wireless course left me as incapable as before of operating the Morse Code was beside the point for we never, from 1941 right into 1945, actually used it. We did indeed use wireless sets, but always in open speech, never needing to descend into Morse Code.

When the time came, early in 1944, to leave our favourite desert, I was surprised to find that I did so with regret. Socially and as a means of developing talents which I had not before realised I possessed, it was a most rewarding period.

The journey back to England, which looked incredibly fresh and green, was heavenly compared with the journey out in 1942. This time it was relatively short, via the Mediterranean on a reasonably comfortable troopship, with plenty of room and proper, reasonably spaced bunks. No repeat of the hell-hole conditions of the voyage out.

Following the pattern of repeating situations that seem to have marked my whole life, the battalion was first quartered in Pembrokeshire, the beautiful county where I have come to live in old age, which was then a main training area for the American forces now coming to Britain in large numbers ready for the D-Day landings in France, and disrupting British life to the point where sayings like 'over-paid, over-sexed and over here' took root. I remember another, based on most American transport being operated by black Americans, 'I don't mind the Americans at all: it is the white fellows with them that I can't stand.'

7
Normandy, and Belgian interlude

For the second time, England was something of an anti-climax on return from the Middle East, as it had been earlier on return from the Far East. Perhaps that is why my memory of this period is less clear than that of the outward journeys.

Anyway, Pembrokeshire was due to get rid of its Americans, whether black or white, very soon, for D-Day was imminent.

Of course, we were fully expecting that, at last, CDL was about to be used for the D-Day landing. Why on earth else had we been sent back to England? But the Americans departed for Utah and Omaha beaches, leaving no trace but a small memorial on the quay at Milford Haven. As usual, we were left behind. Lord Alanbrooke must, once again, have managed to overrule Mr Churchill.

The landing, of course, with the temporary exception of Omaha beach, was a resounding success, in no small measure due to our sister units, the 79th Armoured Division's DD waterproofed tanks and other specialised vehicles. But the British Army was halted before the town of Caen. Yet another opportunity for CDL to make the breakthrough? The possibility must still have been on the cards, for in August 1944 we crossed the Channel en route for Normandy, after only the briefest respite among the green rolling hills of Pembrokeshire. Again the usual exercise of mounting poor old Kite's CDL turret followed, this time in a field in the 'Bocage' country near to Bayeux, in happier times the home of the famous Bayeux tapestry. The site had been the village of Tilly-sur-Seulles, but there was nothing of the village left except the crossroads. All the remains had been just bulldozed out of the way. The Squadron's Scottish Non-Conformist padre said, at Church Parade, how lucky we were to be still in this field, and not at the front, but I think most of the Squadron disagreed with him.

No one could deny that the D-Day landing, whatever its military virtues, was a remarkable feat of organisation and planning. There was the amazing construction project of Mulberry Harbour: an assembly of concrete caissons towed across the Channel and sunk into position to form a breakwater. Mulberry Harbour handled all reinforcements and supplies for the combined British and American forces until our own later efforts on the Island of Walcheren opened up the port of Antwerp. Then there was Pluto, the pipeline under the Channel, which supplied all the allies' fuel requirements for their transport and armoured vehicles in the Normandy bridgehead – an enormous number of vehicles and a prodigious quantity of petrol.

But the real brilliance was shown not in mere technology, but in the subtle field of intelligence. Perhaps the greatest Allied achievement of the whole war was the British breaking of the German secret code, whereby the Allies knew in advance exactly what the German intentions were, but they were fooled completely as to ours.

It was logical to believe that the Allies would attack via the shortest and most convenient route, the mere 22 miles between Dover and Calais. But the Germans did not know about either Mulberry Harbour or Pluto, which made the matter of simple distance less important.

So, when the Allies landed in Normandy, the German High Command thought at first that this attack was only a feint, and the real attack was still to come in the Dover/Calais sector. They were at the time still solidly in control of the whole of Holland, where their powerful XVth Army was stationed. Now, had this army attacked immediately after the Allied landing, when their beachhead was still insecure, they might well have thrown the invaders back into the sea and the whole course of the War turned again in Hitler's favour. Again, one of history's 'might have beens'.

But the German High Command had another very good reason for believing that the real attack was to come in the Pas de Calais area. Yet another colossal deception.

The outspoken American General Patton had for some time been a political embarrassment to the Allies, and had been removed from his command in North Africa, so that he should not further damage the Allied cause. Of course, Patton came into his own again in the final stages of the war, when his penchant for rapid advances became really useful.

But it was a stroke of genius, in the run-up to D-Day, to get the outspoken and troublesome General where he could do no damage, yet further the plans for secrecy as to where the Allies would land, by creating 'Patton's Phantom Army'. So Patton was put in charge of a non-existent army situated in East Anglia, consisting of cardboard tanks, guns, and all the fake paraphernalia of a supposed powerful army in creation.

East Anglia, of course, is far removed from Normandy, and German Intelligence, backed by Luftwaffe aerial observation, reasonably took the evidence of a vast army being created there as additional proof that the Allies meant to attack in the Pas de Calais, or even to the north of that. Such a force could not conceivably be intended for use as far south as Normandy.

So the German High Command was fooled into leaving their powerful XVth Army back in Holland, where they did nothing to stop the true invasion of D-Day in Normandy.

But to return to Tilly-sur-Seulles, it was a strange interlude among the debris of the hotly contested landing battlefields. The 'Bocage' consisted of very small fields divided by high hedges, with, usually, just one gap in the centre. In this gap, all too often, rested the burnt-out skeleton of an American Sherman tank, because, in the gap immediately facing leading into the adjoining field had been one of the deadly German 88mm anti-tank guns and no Sherman could withstand an 88mm or any other German anti-tank missile. We used to say that the Sherman, unlike my poor old Kite, was reasonably reliable mechanically, but might so well have been made of cardboard for all the opposing anti-tank fire it could withstand. So, sadly, the burnt-out tank was all too often accompanied by the five graves of its crew.

It may not be generally known, but tanks were equipped with two kinds of ammunition; high explosive, for general destructive purposes, and solid shot for inter-tank combat. The tank, or anti-tank, shell, would usually have enough force to penetrate the turret armour, but not enough to pierce an exit hole. So what happened was that the shot would ricochet off the inner walls of the turret, almost certainly killing all the crew inside. Hence the graves beside the wrecked tank.

But this was not all that awaited in the Normandy 'Bocage' country. Backing up the attacking tank would be a file of infantry, moving up under cover along the ditch approaching the gap. As soon as the tank had been disposed of, all too often the file of infantry would become victims of machine gun fire, and this led to the most unpleasant job the 11th Battalion RTR was called upon to perform.

For we were the only unit in the area with absolutely nothing else to do and so were the natural choice to be called upon for a burial party. It is strange that, long afterwards, it is the trivial event that lingers in one's memory, while the traumatic one just fades away.

September 1944 in Normandy turned out to be a hot and damp month, with lots of wasps and other insects and conditions conducive to rapid rotting of corpses. The unfortunate soldiers could not have been dead for very long, but already all flesh had disappeared, leaving just sticky, blackened skeletons. So, the self-named 'B Squadron Corpse' had to help collect, and temporarily bury, what remained of the dead infantry. Memory seems to have blotted out completely all record of what should have been a horrific experience.

But events in this fast-moving war quickly caught up with us, for the log jam at Caen duly broke without our help, once again. From then onwards, with the sole exception of the Ardennes offensive in the winter of 1944, everything went the Allies' way. So, naturally, CDL was dumped at last and the 11th Battalion joined the advance across Europe. Indeed, we spearheaded it.

After the breakthrough at Caen events moved with a speed that was limited only by the speed of tanks, and unlike 'Kite' the American Shermans, whatever the quality of their armour, certainly produced a splendid turn of speed, nor was their 75mm gun less than effective at short range.

The American breakthrough in the south of Normandy developed into an encircling movement in which most of the German armies in France were trapped, and many of them utterly destroyed. There was criticism at the time that the 'Falaise Gap' was not closed quickly enough to prevent the escape of most of the Panzer Divisions, but the war in France was effectively over none the less.

Meanwhile the 11th Battalion, still in their field at Tilly-sur-Seulles, grew more and more frustrated at not seeing any of the action and our Squadron authorities, sensing the mood, decided to do something to prevent morale deteriorating. So came the first of our 'sightseeing' trips. We were offered transport to the Falaise Gap, the centre of destruction and, of course, I took advantage of this. Evidently, our guides never found the main area of destruction, but I remember vividly seeing a wrecked German 'Tiger' tank in a ditch with, horrific sight, one of the dead crew beside it, the corpse turning green.

For the last months of the war we were as active as we had previously been inactive. It was our 'Buffalo' amphibious craft, together with those of our sister units, who ferried the assault infantry across every water barrier that lay across the route to the Rhine, and eventually the Elbe.

So I parted from my old friend and adversary 'Kite'. In the end, I was rather sorry to lose the old wreck. Our battalion followed in the Allied advance into Belgium, after a period of only two weeks' training on our new 'steeds' – that is after wasting three years on our CDL tanks. Then we went straight into action, as recorded in the following chapter.

But, first, we had a very pleasant interlude in the village of Rupelmonde, in Flanders, whose claim to fame lay in being the birthplace of the celebrated geographer, Mercator, inventor of Mercator's Projection. Needless to say, his statue adorned the village centre.

Rupelmonde had about as friendly a welcome for us as one would find. At the end of the war the British were incredibly popular in Belgium, I seem to remember that Belgium even offered to become part of the United Kingdom at that time. Now, one wonders, might the whole course of European history have been changed if this offer had been taken up? We might have had a British, instead of a Franco-German dominated European Union.

Of course, the friendly local Flemish speakers were additionally encouraged to find that our battalion contained a large contingent of 'Geordies', hitherto regarded by the rest of the unit as barbarous foreigners who could not even speak English, The Tynesiders suddenly found themselves completely at home. For the Flemings spoke a language basically very similar to their own.

Anyway, linguistically connected or not, the 11th Battalion got on like a house on fire at Rupelmonde, particularly the intellectually oriented like Sergeant Purver, Trooper Myers and myself, who made great friends with an intelligent English-speaking young man who entertained us with the best the village could offer at the time at the local cafe; the revolting 'acorn' coffee. While we discussed the evils of the German occupation, the less informed locals, who mostly wore clogs at that time, hung around on the fringes, trying to be part of the act.

But the Rupelmonde interlude was only a fortnight long, and mostly taken up with intensive training on handling our new 'Buffalo' vehicles.

Here, again, we come to one of history's great 'might-have-beens'.

The Buffalo was just a transport vehicle, but a very unusual one, its great virtue being that it was able, with equal facility, to travel in the water, through the mud fringing the water and on soft dry land – anywhere in fact except on a metalled road. To travel by road it had to be mounted on another specialised vehicle, a tank transporter.

The Buffalo could do this because, like a tank, it was a tracked, not a wheeled vehicle, but it had a very light track with 'cupped' track plates which acted in the water rather like a paddle wheel. This light track also enabled the Buffalo to climb quite steep mud banks, on which wheels could not get a grip, and just span helplessly. It was this remarkable vehicle which spearheaded the Allied advance right across Europe, enabling them to cross every water obstacle *before* the first bridge was built. It was one of the decisive, if little known, weapons of the Second World War.

Looking in profile rather like one of the early tanks of the First World War, the Buffalo was just a hollow box, unarmoured, and made only of light steel, capable of resisting nothing more than a bullet. It was large enough to transport a 'Jeep' or similar small vehicle, a gun or a platoon of infantry with their equipment. All these were embarked and disembarked by means of a ramp which could be raised or lowered by a simple hand wheel and ratchet mechanism. Raising and lowering this ramp was the simple, but all-important function of the former wireless operator of a tank – in other words, this was the main contribution to the Allied war effort of the erstwhile 'B Squadron Corpse'.

The Buffalo was an American invention, originally designed not as a weapon of war at all, but for civilian flood relief in the Mississippi valley. In other words, it was meant just to rescue families trapped in their houses when the mighty Mississippi, 'Ol Man River', staged one of its periodic floods.

So, the Buffalo was already in stock in the United States and did not even have to be specially manufactured. All that prevented it being supplied to the British Army was the political will. And here we enter the rather murky field of inter-Allied wartime politics.

General Montgomery, always a prickly personality, though popular with his rank and file troops, quarrelled with practically all of the other commanders with whom he had to co-operate – and not least with the American Commander in Chief, General Eisenhower.

Montgomery, as it turned out absolutely correctly, wanted to make a single thrust for Berlin, which he would do with the British 2nd

Army; Eisenhower wanted to advance on the whole front, so that the Americans, who inevitably represented the greater numbers, would be seen to have won the war.

So followed one of the heroic and imaginative operations of the war, the Arnhem airborne landing, featured very accurately in Sir Richard Attenborough's excellent film *A Bridge Too Far*. The airborne landing failed in its attempt to exploit the mauling the German Army had just suffered in France, leaving them temporarily with no viable force defending the direct route to Berlin. As with most failures, a combination of circumstances contributed to it. For example, if the British command had paid more attention to the accurate intelligence supplied to them by the Dutch Underground; or if a landing point had been selected nearer to the vital Arnhem Bridge, the result might have been different. As it was, only some 2,000 men out of the whole Airborne Division escaped back across the Neder Rhine, and they were rescued only by old fashioned rowing boats.

Now, if they had had Buffaloes to cross the river, the hard-pressed airborne troops could have been reinforced and probably the river crossing secured so that the British armour, spearheaded by the Guards Armoured Division, could have been in Berlin while the Russian armies were still back in White Russia. Then the war could have ended a year earlier and, perhaps, there would have been no Soviet-dominated Eastern Europe, and no Cold War. Not for the want of a horseshoe nail, but for want of a few Buffaloes, the whole recent history of Europe may have been changed.

But why, one wonders, were there no Buffaloes at the crucial time? They were supplied almost as soon as the British airborne landing had failed and immediately proved their value, as recorded in the following chapter.

One cannot know, but I suspect that this must have been deliberate and done for political reasons, arising out of the jealousy between the British and Americans. The last thing Eisenhower wanted was for Montgomery to be first into Berlin, and, one suspects, the Americans took steps to see that he did not have the hardware to ensure success*.

Anyway, exit CDL and enter the era of the Buffalo. We had a short interlude in Holland where we were quartered, briefly, in the vacated

---

* Another explanation is that Roosevelt, his judgment clouded by approaching death, was fooled by the cunning Stalin into allowing the Russians into Berlin first.

Philip's factory at Eindhoven. It might have been here, though I am now not sure, that I ruined my unblemished military record by using some initiative.

This incident was in very cold and unpleasant weather and might have been about the time of the Germans' last real effort to win the war, their Ardennnes offensive.

I happened to be on guard at our vehicle park on the night in question, guarding our precious Buffaloes. Suddenly, a flight of three fighter aircraft appeared overhead: unmistakably German, and recognisable as their not too successful Focke-Wulfs. I recognised a unique opportunity: a chance actually to fire a gun in anger. I was fired at pretty intensively during the Walcheren operation (see next chapter), but I had not actually fired a gun in response.

Now was my chance. The Buffalo's sole weapon was a 20mm Oerlikon cannon, a very neat and workmanlike gun which I had always longed to try out. There was my target: surely one of the last aggressive fighter patrols the Luftwaffe would launch in this war. Suppose I could actually bring down a German fighter aircraft?

Sadly, or perhaps fortunately, I was not quick enough; before I had them correctly sighted the Focke-Wulfs had gone. They were flying very low, no doubt judging this the safer procedure, and the Oerlikon was considered to be a pretty accurate gun. No doubt, had they hit, its 20mm cannon shells would have done a Focke-Wulf no good at all. But it was all a matter of being quick enough.

I suspect, had I managed to fire, I should at least have been placed on a charge for having fired without orders – or much worse. Supposing I had hit it and the plane had come down on surrounding housing and killed some innocent civilian! Perhaps I should give thanks for having had slow reactions.

And so on to our real task of crossing water obstacles, to the Siegfried Line, and to the last impediment, the Rhine.

8

The Scheldt – our first brush with the enemy

Present day warfare has tended to be an unromantic thing; a matter of timetables, scientific precision, competent handling of supply and the massing of war material on a huge scale. Gone are the days of lost causes, last ditch stands and individual heroics. Such things just do not yield results any more.

However, there were in the second World War some notable exceptions to this general ruling, and of these few none were more notable than the operations connected with the clearing of the Scheldt Estuary, and in particular the epic assault on the little isle of Walcheren. We had been newly equipped at this time to take part in operations scheduled to clear the entrance to the port of Antwerp for Allied shipping; an operation essential if the war were to make any further progress.

Towards this operation the Canadians, before our arrival, had already cleared the greater part of the pocket on the south bank of the Scheldt. The first operation in which the Buffaloes had been used in Europe had been by the Assault Engineers in the seaborne landing on this obstinately-held strip of enemy territory, so we judged, rightly as it transpired, that we were intended for the first landings on the northern shore of the estuary.

It was our first operation, after an incredibly long and dreary spell of waiting and training, our first brush with the opposition. At the prospect our lads were all most elated: at last we were about to get down to the job for which we had come into the Army.

On a grey day in late October we left Sluskil, where we had been quartered in an empty chemical works. This time we did not travel by transporter, but in our own craft via the local canal network, which led into a large main canal leading to the river port of Termugen. This was the same port from which the earlier expedition had embarked, and we used the same parking ground in a large potato field, where we remained until the evening of the next day. There was an atmosphere of uncertainty, of excitement about this expedition which did not apply to the later, full-power attacks of the British

Army. With some of the latter the support was so massive that the result seemed a foregone conclusion. Always one heard the expression 'they haven't a chance'. This was different. We did not know where we were going, but we could guess, and this we knew would be a small sea-borne expedition, of necessity of a size we ourselves could carry. Anything might happen; this was an adventure into the unknown.

Not till a few hours before starting did we find out our precise destination, the island of South Beveland, directly opposite to us on the north shore of the Scheldt. There was a certain amount of changing of plans at the last moment but, on the whole, briefing was fairly clear and to the point. Our Squadron was crossing in two line ahead columns.

On the far shore we should find a broad sandy beach by a steep dyke about 20ft high. The landing point was to be marked with a green light by the first craft to land, and was otherwise to be recognised by a long tongue of land jutting out to the right of it. We were given maps and aerial photographs of the area.

The original intention was for us to climb the dyke and proceed about half a mile inland to deposit our infantry near to their objective, the village of Hoyland. This idea was not at all popular with us, as there seemed to be some doubt as to whether we could climb the formidable dyke in the first place; and furthermore the idea of exploring so far into enemy territory in a vehicle so vulnerable as a Buffalo was not attractive. Everyone was therefore considerably relieved, in spite of the pleasurable excitement worked up by this operation in general, to learn that the plan had been changed. Only one troop was now required to proceed inland; the remainder were now to unload on the beach.

It was additionally pleasant to hear that the opposition was supposed to consist of inferior quality fortress troops, and that they were believed to be almost without artillery at this point. Around 11.00 pm our assault infantry arrived; the 52nd Lowland Division, formerly trained as specialist mountain troops. This was their first action, and we were instructed to conceal the fact that it was also *our* first action and tell boastful tales of our supposed previous sanguinary deeds, in order to buck up their morale. I think this was done fairly satisfactorily, for *our* morale had certainly never been higher than it was on this evening.

We were to make the run with red rear lights burning to facilitate keeping formation and so that nobody should get lost. This idea had its points, but it also turned out to be a source of potential danger later on, and it was never used again. At midnight the two columns moved off and slipped into the murky waters of the Scheldt. It was a black night with low scudding cloud and very poor visibility. Once well out into the estuary the water was quite choppy and we were to all intents and purposes at sea. The estuary here was over ten miles wide and no sign of land could be seen; just the double line of red pinpricks of light disappearing ahead into the unknown, the inky and uninviting waste of water, and a great sense of loneliness.

No one spoke during the trip; they just listened to the steady drone of the engines; shuffling occasionally to make themselves more comfortable with their masses of equipment in the sardine-tight packed vehicle. Our infantry had with them an Alsatian dog, trained to smell out mines, which whimpered occasionally and was fondled into silence by the soldier in charge of it. All eyes tried to pierce the gloom ahead. My craft almost met with disaster when one from the other column missed his way and ran across our path. Suddenly looming up out of nowhere, he crashed right into us. Luckily it was only a glancing blow and, apart from a shock to our passengers, no harm was done. Keeping in formation with these craft is difficult at any time, but in this case it was extremely awkward. There was a strong current running, our line formation was strung out over a tremendous distance, and every so often the head of the column, for reasons we could not fathom, would halt.

A Buffalo has no anchor, and in a current, of course, cannot stand still. The only possible way of halting on a given spot in the water is to run round and round in small circles. Having to repeat this manoeuvre every few minutes soon lost for everyone the craft ahead to whose tail they were supposed to stick at all costs. Several craft had got themselves into the wrong column, and the infantry who had started all sorted out into the correct order in which they were to land were in their wrong formation and hopelessly mixed up. As we neared our destination after about an hour's run, German ack-ack fire began to appear ahead with flares, tracer shells and other outward and visible signs of alarm. It appears that they took the powerful drone of our many engines for an air attack, and reacted accordingly. Not having encountered Buffaloes before, this was a natural mistake for them to make; the sound would be very similar. Indeed, but for our rear lights, I believe a complete surprise would have been achieved, and they would never have known until it was upon them that a landing had taken place.

Finally the column came to a long halt, so long that every vestige of formation was lost, and dozens of craft were milling around in the most hopeless confusion. In doing so they were naturally showing their rear lights to the enemy, which gave the game away. A dark blur away to the right presently revealed itself as the spur of land marking our beach, and it became clear that we had arrived. Whether we were ahead of schedule or what other cause there was for delay in landing I never found out; sufficient to say that it was far too long.

Delays like this at crucial moments, I have found, are most upsetting to a man strung up to the point of excitement he generally reaches before an attack. The suspicion immediately arises in your mind that something has gone wrong, that somewhere among the intricate co-ordination of timing and movement there has been a slip-up which is liable to mean disaster. There is usually no foundation for these indefinite fears, but all the circumstances tended to strengthen them: the darkness, the great stretch of open water at our backs, the enemy coast ahead with we knew not what behind it. It made us feel terribly alone, isolated, abandoned; and it was from such slight and indefinite foundations that fancies among military forces grow and spread. Signs of the spread of such feelings of alarm began to show among our raw infantry; indeed a more trying baptism of fire they could hardly have had.

Eventually we picked out the forbidding dark wall of the dyke ahead of us, and the green landing light marking the beach. My vehicle commander now had not the faintest idea where we were or where we were supposed to be, so decided, in the absence of any definite orders over the wireless, to get ashore on the beach without delay. This we did, landing easily and pulling up on to the gently sloping beach. It turned out that we were quite wrong in doing this; we landed not only before we should, but also on the wrong point of the beach, with the result that our infantry were separated from the rest of their company, and were in a complete fog as to what they should do. As it was, we were among the first craft to land, not more than half a dozen Buffaloes being already drawn up under the shelter of the dyke. My Buffalo commander went in search of the Squadron Commander in the hope of finding out just what was happening.

He was gone some ten minutes, during which time our infantry cargo became increasingly jittery, the situation being in no way helped by the fact that the enemy, ranging on our red lights milling around just off the shore, had at last appreciated what was happening and opened fire with his mortars. Shot after shot came whistling from out of the blackness beyond the dyke and fell with devastating accuracy among the crowded craft clustered at the water's edge, raising fountains of glistening spray against the murky river. That we did not, during this mortaring, sustain heavy casualties was purely a matter of the grace of God.

It was impossible for us to escape entirely so concentrated a hail of fire, however, and after a few minutes one craft sustained a hit directly amidships. Oddly enough, it was the only craft there which did not belong to us: it was one of the Assault Engineers' craft, our sister Buffalo unit, and should not have been there at all, but on the second landing beach some distance away. There was a bright flash, and instantaneously the whole craft was enveloped in a sea of flame as its petrol tanks exploded. The water and beach for hundreds of yards around were lit up with flickering light. I saw two members of the crew scramble out at lightning speed over the doomed Buffalo's bows, only to find that the water, now covered with blazing petrol, was itself alight. She burned for what seemed to the frightened watchers to be ages, but was probably not more than 5 minutes in fact, and eventually sank completely out of sight.

This incident was the most shattering experience of its kind that had yet fallen to my lot, and I believe that others present were similarly affected. It had been proved that it *could* happen, and while the light of the fire illuminated the confused scene, we felt as naked and exposed as if held in a spotlight. Lit up as we were, it did not seem possible that further shots could miss us, and never in my life did I feel so thankful as when the fire at last died down, then flickered out, allowing the protecting darkness to envelop us once more.

As so often happened, however, the enemy neglected to press his advantage while he had it, to his fatal cost, and shortly afterwards the succession of screaming missiles ceased, and again all was peace except for the steady throb of engines. Warfare at night, as this incident showed, can be most frightening. You are frightened of the unknown the darkness conceals, and even more frightened when its protecting pall is temporarily lifted. This, however, was the evening's climax and no one else was hit, those vehicles which went inland over the dykes likewise returning unscathed.

Our vehicle commander eventually returned with instructions to discharge our infantry where we were, and rather unwillingly, they eventually climbed out, the enormous amount of gear that infantry carries following them out by degrees. Upon looking round the craft after they had gone I found left behind one collapsible bicycle, 4 shovels, 2 picks, one case of mortar bombs, 1 rifle, 1 entrenching tool, a number of clips of ammunition, 1 bayonet and several pieces of individual equipment and clothing, all of which goes to demonstrate part of the reason why war costs so much. The whole issue I dumped over the side where we were, with the exception of ammunition, which went into the Scheldt on the way back.

Having unloaded, we soon afterwards received instructions to clear off out of the way, a course we were not sorry to follow. That beach had become a place where no one cared to linger longer than was absolutely necessary. We backed out, turned, and made back towards the other shore where our collecting area lay somewhat lower down the estuary from Termeugen. Our commander had been told, though the rest of the crew had not, the precise route to be taken; nevertheless before we had long passed the jutting tongue of land, and the menacing coast line had faded into the gloom, we were hopelessly lost.

It was now getting light, but a heavy mist still hung over the Scheldt, and once having lost the way there was no definite means of finding it again. Our craft were fitted with compasses, but only one in the squadron had his adjusted and in working order, so we had no help there.

Our artillery had now opened up from the mainland and the German guns were beginning to fire from all directions. Our craft, alone on the wide estuary of the Scheldt, surrounded by grey, choppy water and drenched by showers of spray had ceased to be at all a pleasant place to be in at dawn on this inhospitable coast. We ran round in circles until all sense of direction was lost, and we might have been heading back towards the enemy coast for all we knew to the contrary. Gunfire seemed to come from every direction. When we started off I had, myself, a fair idea of the way we should go, but since then our crazy course left me as confused as our Buffalo commander appeared to be. Where we might have landed up Providence alone knows had we not spotted another Buffalo, which turned out to be one of the Assault Engineers' craft heading back to the same assembly area. This craft we followed in without further incident, duly sighting the lighted pylon we should have found for ourselves. A gap had been bulldozed in the dyke here (not such a tall dyke as on the German side) and ran into our assembly area, beautifully laid out in taped lines, and with a generously stocked petrol dump at the entrance. Breakfast was laid on at 7 o'clock, and by this time most of our craft had returned. We reorganised and checked up the craft, after which nothing happened until the afternoon, when we loaded up some more infantry, and made the trip again. The crossing looked vastly different in daylight, though even under a clear sky still depressing. The low muddy banks skirting South Beveland were now shrouded with smoke from artillery fire, and the rattle of Bren and Spandau sounded from the distance. A gap had now been bulldozed through the dyke here also; a few naval craft lay off the shore but the beach seemed generally quiet and deserted. There was no enemy fire at this time.

I only made the two trips across the grey and muddy Scheldt estuary. We were to have made two more that day, each time moving up to the loading area in readiness, but our craft was not required. That night we indulged in blessed uninterrupted sleep. After lunch next day some dozen of our craft were detailed to get ready to move for another job – what it might be no one knew. Again in line ahead, we re-entered the river, this time heading upstream, and crossing a number of shoals and sandbanks, of which there are many bordering this shallow estuary.

This being a clear day, the South Beveland coast could be seen plainly. The part of the island opposite to us was covered by a long smoke screen, apparently protecting the flank of our forces. Our artillery was still firing at intervals, but there now seemed little German counter fire.

Eventually we reached a small bay from which led a very steep stone-lined slipway over the dyke. Somewhat to our surprise all vehicles climbed up here without difficulty, parking up for the night on the road above. Torrential rain followed; however, as this time we had a good tarpaulin sheet we spent a comfortable night sleeping in the vehicle. A sheeted-up Buffalo, so long as it is sheeted *before* the inside is wet, makes a satisfactory, and, under static conditions, even a comfortable home. The trouble arises when the floor is already wet, and one is still obliged to find a place to lie down. Since these early days we learned on many occasions to value our mobile homes, and to dread above anything the prospect of losing them. No old-time cavalry man was ever more miserable at the loss of his horse than we were when we lost our Buffaloes.

The next morning we were straightaway loaded up on transporters, and moved off in the mid morning, to the accompaniment of occasional shots from the battery of 5·5 inch medium artillery in the neighbouring field, still pounding away across the Scheldt at South Beveland. There was much speculation as to our eventual destination, but when we crossed again into Belgium, making for the coast, there was little doubt as to where we could be bound.

9
Walcheren – our Commando operation

When we reached Ostend in the evening, it became clear that this was to be a seaborne expedition, and where could such an expedition be headed at such a time but the guardian island of Walcheren, the key to the Scheldt, to Antwerp, to the supply of the Allied armies, and to the winning of the whole war?

We stayed in Ostend for two full days, leaving in the afternoon of the third; two delightful days in the former German barracks now used as a transit camp, and a positive haven of luxury beside our late standards. We slept in a somewhat draughty barrack room, which had, however, double decker bunks, an unheard-of luxury. This establishment had civilians working, and also serving food, which was, by Army standards, excellent and almost unlimited in quantity. We passed our two days in pleasant freedom, having a good bath and haircut, looking round the town, eating black market delicacies in the fantastically expensive cafes*, and in visiting cinemas again.

The little resort looked somewhat overcast by war conditions, but still displayed a rather threadbare gaiety. The boarding houses along the front were barred off by barbed wire and converted, with the addition of concrete, into a solid fortification. The front had been considerably battered, the broken rubble from it still lay about in quantities. The neighbourhood of the promenade was completely deserted. Not many people were about in the main streets; those that were being of the cosmopolitan type that always has inhabited the Channel ports. Large numbers of shops were closed, but those still open were fairly well stocked with luxury goods. Fruit, in particular, was plentiful if expensive.

The town in general looked rather out of date, a little drab, a little tawdry and somehow a little pathetic. An expression of gay,

---

* It needs to be borne in mind that soldiers on active service overseas had nothing to spend their money on. There was just nothing to buy – particularly food – over most of Europe. Also, being a non-smoker and non-drinker, I was better off than the majority.

irresponsible, pre-war shallowness, it hung uncertainly waiting for the life that sustained it to return. Over the suspended animation of the town itself flowed a full, vigorous tide of militarism. All traffic was military, and soldiers filled all the pavements. Ostend at this time, inadequate as it was for the purpose, was an important British base. There were men being returned to England, naval men, Belgian and Dutch army men, dapper and exquisite French officers, Czechs, Poles, Jugo-Slavs; every type and nationality of the Allied armed forces.

Everywhere was the buzz of military preparation, and the subdued yet super-charged atmosphere that heralds the birth of an important enterprise, and a dangerous one. The docks were fenced off with barbed wire and were filled to capacity with small naval craft. Large piles of stores could be seen heaped on the quays; lorries and transporters continuously discharged more stores and vehicles. Prominent among the soldiers thronging the streets were lithe, clean cut young men walking with long swinging strides, clad in camouflage battle jackets and green berets – Commandos; a further indication of the difficult nature of this job. Clearly it was only a small scale operation, but equally clearly it was to pack the most powerful punch possible for a force of its size.

On the afternoon of the second day we were called out to load our vehicles, which had been left parked on the quayside, on to tank landing craft waiting in the dock. Twenty-nine LCTs lay parked side by side with their ramps down, and we ran straight aboard; 3 vehicles to a craft. Prior to this we had embarked our own loads. Most of us had ammunition, petrol, and various stores with us; some, of which my own was one, had hospital equipment and medical stores. We also had to carry 14 Canadian medical orderlies. Several carried 'Weazels'; our smallest amphibious craft, so that when we put to sea some LCTs resembled those box bricks which fit one into another; in the water was the LCT which carried Buffaloes, which in turn carried Weazels; all being capable of taking to the water on their own account.

This expedition, as we watched it embarking, was surely the most specialised in proportion to the forces employed. Flail tanks were there, petards and flame-thrower tanks for coping with pill-boxes, all kinds of amphibious craft, the indispensable bulldozers, naval rocket boats; practically everything but artillery and conventional infantry forces. All the actual ground combat troops attached to our part of the expedition were three troops of Commandos. Personnel manning this accumulation of mechanical equipment were as various as the equipment itself. The tank units were British, the medical services and bulldozers Canadian. The LCTs were Navy craft, and naval men were otherwise considerably mixed up in all sorts of other jobs. The commandos were Royal Marines.

As a seaborne landing, this was primarily a naval, or rather a combined operation, in which the Navy controlled and the Army played a subsidiary part, and the difference in atmosphere from an ordinary Army operation was marked. A certain absence of fuss and palaver, a carefree abandon that did not in any way detract from efficiency, a preoccupation with getting the job itself done, rather than with the way it was done.

This was the atmosphere that lay like a mantle over the little port of Ostend. When all was stowed away in readiness, we departed again to relax in comfort while we could, for a farewell meal or visit to the cinema.

Towards 5 pm on the afternoon of the next day we collected our kit and blanket rolls, and drove by lorry down to the docks. The LCTs were parked side by side against the wharf, our own being some six places away, so that it was necessary to climb over the intervening craft in order to reach it. As crews of the Buffaloes we should have been aboard early, before our passengers arrived; but we were kept hanging about on the wharf for over two hours, being moved about at intervals when we were in someone else's way. This mess-up was due apparently to our officer in charge having entered the dock by the wrong entrance, thus missing the naval officer directing embarkation. Mismanagement of this type dogged the direction of our particular part in the operation from first to last.

The B Squadron vehicles were attached to 79 Squadron of the Assault Engineers, another Buffalo unit, for this operation, and under their command. It was not until waiting on the wharf to embark that we met the officer under whose instructions we were supposed to be working and received briefing instructions, such as they were.

My vehicle and one other from my own troop under the command of a sergeant were operating separately as hospital craft. In effect, we were to be ambulances. All our sergeant received by way of briefing was an aerial photograph of the landing point, a map of our sector for each craft and the valediction 'Good Luck; I might be seeing you somewhere on the beach.'

The photograph and map were of Westkapelle on the, then, island of Walcheren, scene of a military mess-up of the 17th century recorded in the satirical rhyme 'Great Chatham with his sabre drawn was waiting for Sir Richard Strachan. Sir Richard, longing to be at 'em, was waiting for the Earl of Chatham.' Since the war, the geography of the region has been altered by incorporation of the island of Walcheren into the mainland, as part of the operation of draining the former Zuyder Zee, but back in 1944 it was indeed an island.

Fortunately, perhaps, I was about the only one present who knew of the unfortunate historical precedent for a combined naval and military operation on Walcheren.

The island was roughly diamond shaped, and consisted of an absolutely flat plain, practically the whole of which was below sea level, retained by a high sand dyke. Some weeks earlier the RAF had blown two large gaps in this dyke: at the western point of the diamond at Westkapelle, and another near to the southern point of Flushing. Through these gaps the sea rushed, flooding the whole interior of the island to a depth of several feet. Only a small area around Middelburg in the centre was unflooded. It was really quite a small island, only some twelve miles across. The dyke from the northern apex of the island beyond the village of Domburg to the neighbourhood of Flushing had been built up into a solid line of concrete fortifications, forming one of the strongest parts of the Atlantic wall, and housing an immense number of guns of every calibre.

Without doubt the enemy's capacity for resistance had been undermined by his losing all his communications across the island and all inland supply dumps; but otherwise it was as strong a position as any defence line possibly could be. Our only real advantage lay in the poor quality of the enemy garrison, which consisted of the Germans' 'white bread division', which comprised solely men with stomach complaints. Such was the position we were to attack. Two attacks were being launched, one at Flushing and one at Westkapelle, the gaps being used in either case to enable our amphibious craft to penetrate behind the dyke. The LCTs were carrying us right up to the beach bordering the gap, where they were to drop us, and we were to carry on through the gap under our own power. In the case of my own craft, we were to land our hospital equipment and staff on the beach to the south side of the gap; the site for the hospital being upon the first prominent hillock of the dyke. Such was the theory of it; as will be seen later things did not quite work out.

However, to return to the quayside, where a crowd of Buffalo men were left wearily sitting about. At last, after everyone else had been aboard some time, we received instructions to board our craft, which operation involved climbing over five extremely crowded craft lying between. We found our 14 medical orderlies in charge of a Major, RAMC, already aboard our Buffalo, and amused ourselves watching the preparation for moving off. Darkness had now descended, and it was a black night. The usual degree of confidence in our immunity from German air attack was shown, however, in the fairly plentiful dock and harbour lighting, outlining in dark silhouette the shapes of the numerous small craft alive with preparation.

Towards midnight the 29 LCTs and their fleet of attendant small craft slipped smoothly and silently out, the dull glow of light faded behind us and the little fleet was alone in the darkness, bound for who could say what. We drank our tins of self-heating soup, a marvellous invention for these occasions, and settled to doze as comfortably as we could. It was neither comfortable nor warm enough for proper sleep, however, and I hardly lost consciousness among the litter of recumbent forms on our Buffalo. Nights such as this are long and exhausting indeed. Dawn, when it broke at last, brought a fair day with clear sky at first, becoming slightly hazy later on, and clouding over with cirrus towards evening.

Our little fleet looked extremely beautiful against the blue sky and pale sunlight of early morning. With the LCTs in two lines ahead, and the various small naval craft scattered around them, they covered a wide stretch of sea. Breakfast to all on board was served from the LCT's rations, so that our own compo ration (which might need to last a long time) should not be broken into, and shortly afterwards we sighted land. This long low tongue jutting out into the sea I at once recognized, from previous acquaintance, as Flushing harbour.

Immediately behind hung a pall of thick smoke, from which I gathered that the attack had already gone in. Clearly we had not long to go now; an hour at the most would see us at our objective. Presently three long low shapes appeared on the western horizon, one of them massive-looking with towering superstructure. This I rightly guessed to be that time-honoured bombardier of coastal fortifications, the old battleship *Warspite*, veteran of Zebrugge in the First World War. With her were two monitors and several attendant smaller craft. She looked a colossus of power, as every few moments a huge cloud of black smoke belched from her side as a salvo started on its journey shoreward.

We afterwards found out that *Warspite* was not by any means happy in that position. She was expecting the heavy coastal guns at Knocke in the pocket south of the Scheldt estuary to open up on her, but most fortunately this, the last heavy battery in the area, had just previously been captured by the Canadians. As the *Warspite* and her consorts faded from sight into the morning haze, her target, and our objective, came into view. I saw first a billowing smoke cloud merging into the general haziness of the eastern horizon, which gradually clarified into a firm line of low sandhills, covered in a smoky haze and pin-pointed with sharp white gun flashes.

My craft carrying supplies, and not assault troops, was naturally well back in the column, and by the time we could see the shore clearly the landing craft were already approaching it. The cloud of naval small craft, rocket ships and others, were moving up to engage. Behind us *Warspite* had now ceased firing. The scene before us was blurred and confused and it was difficult to pick out details, but the distance separating us from the smoking shore was fast diminishing. Big water spouts from falling shells began to appear amongst the craft, growing more and more frequent as we drew in. It became plain that this was a really sticky situation, and though I had fully realised that it would be so beforehand, the demonstration of the fact still arrived as a nasty shock. We settled ourselves in our Buffalo, put on tin hats, and kept ourselves down as far as the large load of medical stuff would allow us.

Ahead I spotted a sinking LCT. It was lying low in the water and listing badly. As we left it behind men could be seen jumping over the side like a shower of apples dropping from the tree, while another LCT moved in to pick up the survivors. I did not see the final moment, but her side was badly holed, and she must have sunk. As we moved in I counted four more sinking LCTs. If the LCTs, comparatively easy targets, were suffering, their plight was as nothing to that of the small naval craft, which were charging close in to the beaches to discharge their rockets, or engage the batteries with gunfire. The situation was becoming too tense for exact observation of details, but the smoking wrecks of many of these gallant little craft were fast disappearing into the cold and uninviting North Sea. At about this stage the impression grew that we should be extremely lucky if we penetrated this devastating curtain of fire; it might be our turn any time now, for not one craft, or a few, but practically all, seemed to be meeting with disaster. It was a chastening thought, though I still found difficulty in identifying myself with this orgy of destruction that was going on around us.

I ceased to take much interest in the general scene as a big waterspout appeared close off the starboard of our craft; the matter of keeping one's head down seemed to have become more important, and I concentrated on preparing my mind for the inevitable and see that I was ready to act when it happened.

No further clear impressions struck me until I realised a moment or two later that we were almost upon the line of sand hills. The realisation was a shock; evidently we had weathered the worst of the storm. At least, so I was thinking when a further half dozen waterspouts appeared immediately around us. We were near the guns here and we could hear the whine of the shells overhead and explosions of discharge as well as impact.

Close to our port side the next craft was also carrying Buffaloes; and one of these had a Weazel aboard. At this moment confidence received a further setback; there was a crash and sheet of flame as this Weazel received a direct hit just before we grounded and the LCT's ramp was dropped. I did not see or realise what happened next, my whole attention being absorbed by the movements of my own craft; but I had the story afterwards from the sergeant commanding this particular Buffalo.

Apparently his crew scattered from the blazing vehicle, one of them being severely wounded by the explosion, and the driver going to his assistance. This sergeant stuck to his vehicle and drove it off with its blazing cargo aboard, then dived overboard and swam for it as his Buffalo with the Weazel inside burnt out. By doing so he undoubtedly saved his LCT and the other two vehicles carried by it. On the recommendation of the commander of the LCT he was awarded the Military Medal for this fine and prompt action.

We met him several days later in Westapelle, none the worse for wear, but wearing a Commando beret and possessing only the battledress he stood up in by way of kit. This particular LCT carried the man hit by the explosion and the man who went to his assistance back to Ostend. The former died on the landing craft.

While this was going on to our flank, however, I was fully absorbed in our most spectacular beaching. As soon as the LCT dropped its landing flap, indeed before it was fully down, our driver was off the mark like a runner to the starting gun. The instant the flap touched the ground he was clear of it, and we were tearing through the wide gap, together with our consorts. We were through, and automatically the greatest fury of firing ceased for the simple reason that we were now inside the perimeter of guns, and the larger among them, with their embrasures facing seawards, could not be traversed round to fire inland. It was the same tale as at Singapore over again, when our guns were facing out to sea, while the Japanese were attacking from inland.

We charged forward through shallow water for a few hundred yards, then all vehicles halted where they were, scattered all over the area immediately inside the gap, and I had a chance during this comparative lull to take stock of the situation. The gap itself, through which the sea surged strongly, would have been some 200 yards wide at the mouth. On the left, or northern side, a low sand spit ran up to the utterly smashed and ruined town of Westkapelle, the larger part of it under water. The seaward end of the town consisted just of heaps of rubble; anything the bombers had missed had evidently been flattened by *Warspite*. At the landward end of the main street some houses still stood, dominated by a high round tower whose original purpose I never discovered, but which was now evidently being used as an observation and sniping post. At this time its upper part was on fire, and blazing fiercely. Several more fires burned in the town. To the front of the town between it and our position lay a large bed of reeds.

To our front, stretching as far as the eye could see, was a vast stretch of water, with an occasional tree, house or hedgetop protruding from its surface. In the immediate forefront, and covering most of the angle between the two shores, was a large minefield marked by poles interconnected by wiring. Every third or fourth pole, I noticed, had an anti-personnel mine attached to the top of it, in addition to what might be under the water's surface. A touch on any of these poles by our most unmaneouvrable craft would have set one of these off, with catastrophic consequences.

On the south side of the gap, the line of the dyke appeared much as it had from the seaward side: a ridge of low sandhills gradually growing higher as they faced into the distance. So far as was apparent, the defences here had not been bombarded and were at this stage intact. The first hill rising from the flat beach (the objective for our hospital) had apparently been captured, but there was no evidence of further progress as yet. A big gun was firing from a commanding hillock in the background. To our rear, and moored in a row, were five sound LCTs against the sand spit bordering the gap. Further to the left the bows of one sunken one protruded from the sea.

Just how many LCTs landed safely I never exactly found out. All that I *saw* myself were those just mentioned and a further two mined on the seaward side of the sandhills However, I presume that more craft than this out of the original 29 must have landed safely and pulled out before my craft arrived, for it seemed that all of the Commandos and our Buffalo force had made it; though most of the mechanical equipment was lost. Some half dozen Buffaloes had drawn up on the beach below the future hospital site; some were in a rough line ahead pointing towards the inland end of the town, ourselves being to the rear of this group; and the remainder were scattered about over the wide area immediately inside the gap.

The lull following upon our successful penetration of the gap was not of long duration. After some ten minutes the enemy again had some of his guns trained upon us and the water among our craft rose thickly in towering waterspouts. A Buffalo is a small target for artillery, but in our present position we were sitting birds. Some craft moved slightly to try to better their positions, but there was absolutely no cover available; we were the ducks at a shooting gallery. The position was not bettered for several craft by their having bogged down on mud banks. As I watched, one of our sea-blue craft was hit amidships and, as always with the Buffalo, immediately became a roaring furnace. She carried ammunition, and exploded at intervals with showers of sparks, sending great tongues of flame skywards. Witnessing the end of this craft, no one would have believed it possible that any human being could have emerged alive, yet there was not one casualty aboard her. The entire crew of five scrambled out and made their way to the Westkapelle shore, suffering from nothing more than shock.

After this first casualty the enemy's gunfire improved; in no time the whole area was littered with sinking Buffaloes, and churned by the waterspouts of near misses. Another of our craft burst into flames, and another; at one period four were burning at once, and one was sinking from a mine burst. The second craft to meet disaster was the only one to sustain serious casualties. When she was hit the man in the open back was blown clean out into the water, while the two in the driving cab were trapped inside. The rather unpopular officer commanding this craft then performed the one fine action that did much to raise his reputation. He remounted the blazing vehicle, and at the cost of nasty burns on his arms and hands succeeded in extricating his driver, whose foot had been trapped under the gear box. The wireless operator, who might or might not have been dead beforehand, was burned to a cinder.

I was fortunate in being spared the sight of this tragic episode. The effect on the other two members of the crew was vastly divergent, and serves to illustrate how great a difference is made by individual temperament in cases like these. One, a jolly little Lancashireman, always bubbling over with high spirits, seemed to skate unconcernedly over the whole episode, and showed no after effects at all. The other, a rather serious and over-conscientious youth, was dazed for days afterwards, and indeed never seemed fully to recover from the shock. The effect of this wholesale holocaust upon the remainder was not too cheering, though no shells were falling at this time towards the head of the column. It seemed that it was merely a matter of time before the whole lot of us were picked off one by one, and I was conscious of a desperate anxiety to get moving. It is surprising how, in such circumstances, one takes comfort in the slightest and most inadequate bit of cover.

Of course, those of us who were somewhat removed from the scene of catastrophe did not realise at the time that casualties among so many wrecked craft had been so few. On seeing them go up no one would have believed it possible for anyone to emerge again. Shortly after the various wrecks had finished burning the south side of the beach was apparently deemed secure, for all surviving Buffaloes in the area of destruction moved up and beached under the shelter of the dyke, leaving the water behind them littered with gaunt and blackened skeletons of twisted metal.

Still watching the south side, I saw files of Commandos returning towards the small area at the tip of the dyke which was firmly in their hands. Evidently their first attack along the dyke had been repulsed. I watched them re-form and move off for another attempt. It was already past the time appointed for the establishment of our hospital on the first hill, but clearly progress was well behind schedule. Shortly after this, the column of vehicles nearer to the north side of the gap, mine among them, moved off in the direction of the end of the Westkapelle main street and, eventually reaching this point, we stopped in a semi sheltered position among the outlying houses, where several small trees added a little protection. Actually, of course, this place was no safer than where we had been before, but you always feel better if you have just partial cover from view. In this position we stayed for the remainder of the day. During the afternoon we were fairly continuously under fire here apparently from several directions. We huddled down as far inside the craft as possible, but with the considerable amount of gear already almost filling it there was little enough room for close upon 20 men.

There was a sniper firing low over our heads at intervals, apparently from the clump of reeds mentioned before; it appeared to be a 20 mm gun firing bursts from an unidentified direction (it is remarkable how difficult it is sometimes to judge from what direction fire is coming) and a small artillery piece lobbing shells only some 50 yards ahead of my Buffalo, each shell sending up a small column of water. The last mentioned seemed to have our position fixed, and I was fully expecting each shell to mean 'curtains' for us. At the most optimistic estimate I was not relishing a swim in the cold, dirty, wire-and-mine-strewn water. However, Providence was still with us, for the gunner did not alter his range, though his shells were falling most accurately almost upon the identical spot each time.

While this, and much other, firing was in progress, we saw some Commandos searching for snipers among the reeds covering the approaches to the village, and of necessity wading deep in the water in order to do so. It was here, while the shelling was at its height, that I heard one of the Canadian medical orderlies make what I should consider to be one of the immortal remarks of the war, 'Look at those poor Commandos,' he said, 'wading up to their waists in water,' and he watched them with compassion in his eyes, oblivious to the stream of fire passing narrowly over his own head.

They were a grand collection, this little group of Canadians. Just ordinary, quiet, peaceable men who had not wanted to come on this expedition and did not pretend that they enjoyed it, but being there, bore themselves gallantly. Afterwards, everybody concerned was unanimous in praising the Canadian medical unit. Throughout the bombardment they just lay under such scanty cover as the Buffalo offered, talking little, moving less, absolutely calm and collected. Coolest of all, indeed he seemed to be enjoying himself, was the medical Major in charge under whose instructions we were operating. He was a middle-aged man, stoutish, with round, beaming, moon-like face and spectacles; calm, placid and with a gentle smile. His only worry was what might have happened to his next-in-command, a captain, who was left alone, owing to the failure to clear the hospital site, to cope with all the wounded at his first aid post on the beach. It later transpired that this latter officer had been carrying on all day though wounded himself in the early stages.

Somewhere about this time it occurred to us that our Red Cross pennant flying from the wireless aerial might be drawing fire, and we took it down. Whether or not this had any connection with the fire moving off our craft, I cannot say; however, from whatever cause the firing died down gradually as the afternoon wore on. Towards sunset, when the sky was clear and bright, we saw the finest spectacle of the campaign, and one of the most cheering sights I have ever seen. It was a convincing demonstration of our invincible air-power, and it settled beyond all doubt the issue of this expedition, which up to that point stood in possible risk of failure.

We, from our excellent observation post, suddenly noticed the Commandos retreating again from the disputed southern arm of the dyke, and shortly after the air filled with circling and diving Typhoons. Never did these trusty planes serve Britain more effectively. Selecting their targets, they circled, dived low, and we heard the hissing sound of discharging rockets followed by great clouds of black smoke rising from many scattered points along the dyke. Time and again they circled and dived, finishing off with a bomb after all the rockets had been fired, and returning yet again to machine-gun. I lost all sense of time in watching this exhilarating spectacle, but for probably an hour the sky against the afternoon sun was nothing but diving planes, swishing rockets, little black bombs sailing slowly downwards, and the smoke of explosions rising from smashed pillboxes and gun emplacements. When they had finished not a sound, not a whisper of opposition was to be seen or heard; all was as silent as if war had never come to this ruined island.

Later on we heard, though our position prevented us from seeing, the same process being completed on the northern arm of the dyke behind Westkapelle. The Commandos had little more trouble on the south side, and not so much on the northern side until they approached the next village of Domburg.

At nightfall all our craft in the area moved further down into the main street of the town, where some of the houses were reasonably intact and afforded some cover. We tied up to the front garden railings of the houses to prevent the craft drifting and cooked our evening meal, the first food since breakfast for most of us. The only event of interest before nightfall was the appearance of two tanks proceeding up the street, the only two of our tanks that I saw on the island. Our bulky craft was blocking the street, and some argument and considerable manoeuvring had to take place before they passed us. I presume they were moving up to take part in the attack towards Domburg. As dusk fell we settled down for the night; that is to say we fixed our tarpaulin over the craft and redistributed ourselves as far as possible so that we could rest. However, there was no room for anyone even to lie down properly; some sat, some lay on top of each other, and it was impossible to do more than doze fitfully. I think it was the most cramped and uncomfortable night I have ever spent, and the arrival of dawn was blessed relief, though we had not slept properly for so long.

This next morning again dawned fair, and with the curious post-battle atmosphere of quiet and serenity. One knew by instinct that the worst was already over.

We did not move until mid-morning, so we were able to have a breakfast in peace, and a much needed wash. All this, of course, had to be done in relays upon the small foredeck of the craft. We were just a tiny human island in this waterlogged land, in which all the permanent dwellings were flooded to the first floor at least. Our floating island was our one and only home, and our prison. Unfortunately I must report, as a truthful chronicler, that a certain amount of looting of the abandoned Dutch houses was included in the morning's activities. It was easy to climb from the Buffaloes to the unflooded first floors. When we moved, in single line, ahead, there was a stronger tide running than the previous day. The dyke on the north side was now, we heard, clear as far as the next village, and we could plant our badly needed hospital where it should have been by midday of the previous day. To do this we had to cross the big minefield lying across the gap, threading our way carefully among the minecapped poles.

It was a most nerve-racking journey, this: I found it even more unpleasant than the previous day's shelling. Every so long there would be some hold-up in the column ahead, causing us to slow down. This in turn caused the craft to wobble, pass temporarily out of control, and tend to drift towards those poles with their deadly little anti-personnel mines tied to the tops. Everyone made the passage without accident, though once again it was only owing to chance that it was so. I drew a long breath of relief when we reached the wreckage-strewn beach on the far side. We immediately unloaded our hospital staff and all their paraphernalia, and then made our way to a beach higher up, where we parked under the shelter of the dyke. This spot remained our headquarters for the remainder of the campaign. That afternoon we made the first of a number of journeys up to the first village along the dyke, which had now been captured. We carried our medical equipment and staff to establish a field dressing station there. The flood water reached almost to the base of the dyke along its entire length, leaving in some places sufficient level ground to make a rough Buffalo track; in other places there was not room and we had to turn off into the water, following taped lanes which had been laid by the first craft exploring the way and, they not having hit any mines, presumed to be mine free.

On one of these detours we, in common with several other craft, became 'bellied' in shallow water, and a complicated sequence of tows took place. The fact that many of us had by now lost our tow-ropes did not make things easier. This route of ours along the base of the dyke, sometimes on soft sand, sometimes through water over bomb craters, light railway lines and miscellaneous wreckage from smashed fortifications, was about the most uncomfortable to travel that it would be possible to devise, a sort of natural fairground scenic railway embodying every sort of hazard imaginable. A Buffalo is far from being the world's most comfortable form of transportation at the best of times: it rocks and jerks and bounces like a bucking bronco; but on this particular rough-rider's course it gave us, and the wounded we later transported, one of the roughest rides on record.

Along this route we passed the now silent and deserted gun emplacements, put out of action by the previous day's activities of those heaven-sent Typhoons. Some of these little forts built into the sand of the dyke housed 6" guns and were roofed with concrete fully 6ft thick. They were cracked wide open, as if the massive concrete had been eggshell. The enormous strength of these fortifications, and the miraculous power of the rockets that had destroyed them, alike filled one with awe. It seemed that the irresistible force that could move the immovable object had arrived at last.

I managed at various times to look around several of these gun positions and the dugout and living quarters attached to them. In them was every evidence of the Reich that was supposed to last for a thousand years: comfortable furniture, even curtains, carpets, huge stocks of food and drink. During the day, though fierce fighting was still going on around Domburg on the northern coast, all was quiet on our sector: no shells fell near and we gained the impression, a little premature as it turned out, that all was over bar the shouting. The only disturbance was caused by our engineers blowing up mines on the beach behind our parking station. We had to be careful of this, for the explosions sent showers of shrapnel down on our side of the dyke.

In the evening our craft, with several others, was detailed as ambulance. We were to collect the wounded from the forward areas then some distance past our first village and bring them back to the field dressing station we had set up. Our switchback sand track, difficult by day, was perfectly terrible by night; it was a trying job for the drivers. The Engineer Officer in charge of our activities appeared for the first time since the landing for this job: he guided us up to the spot where we were supposed to find our wounded, but they proved elusive. We kept probing forward, until we were sure that we had gone too far and were among the German lines. It was very eerie in the darkness, with the fortified dyke to one side of us, the great waste of water to the other and we knew not what ahead. Eventually, however, we did find the right place.

During the journey occurred one of those strange incidents with which the war abounded. The RAMC sergeant we had aboard dismounted on one occasion to ask the way, and walked in the darkness straight into a German officer. Being unarmed, he had no idea what to do; neither, apparently, had the German. Both parties decided to leave well alone, the sergeant returning to report the incident and the enemy officer walking on into the gloom. We never heard what happened to him: he just vanished into the night as he had come. Surely this incident illustrates the artificiality of modern war. On coming face to face with a supposed enemy, neither knew just what to do.

After a short wait we loaded up two stretcher cases and some ten walking wounded, several of them apparently in a serious condition. Then back we went, crashing and bumping over the frightful track; our wounded did not complain, though it must have been a terribly painful journey for them. We improvised what seats we could for them and what else we could to make our appalling ambulance bearable. A shower of rain came on during the journey back and we had to sort out what groundsheets we could to cover them. Still, for them, it was our Buffaloes or nothing, for no wheeled vehicle on earth could have passed that way. The final and crowning discomfort for them was being obliged partly to climb and partly to be lifted over the side of the craft, as our vehicle had no working let-down ramp.

The dressing station, in charge of the colonel commanding the medical detachment, had been set up in the village school. It was not a large room, and by the time we had emptied our Buffaloes we were parking stretchers in the corridors outside. What a strange little hospital this was! There were not enough medical orderlies to carry in all the stretchers, so each of our crews carried in its own, and helped in the walking wounded. All the floor space, and the tops of the miniature children's desks were covered by stretchers, while the less serious cases sat in corners and cubby holes. Only one oil lamp illuminated this surgeon's labours, his operating table was a child's desk, and he worked to the accompaniment of intermittent groans from the smashed and broken men, who only such a short time ago had walked so jauntily along the quay at Ostend.

When we had done what we could for the wounded, we were told to stand by in case any more should arrive, but that in the meantime we might sleep. So the vehicles were sheeted up where we stood in the village street, and we snatched a precious three hours' sleep, our first 'lie down' sleep since the operation began. Before light we were rousted out again, to take a load of wounded, now fit to be moved, back to our base hospital. These lads were even more unfortunate than our last lot, for this time we slipped into a bomb crater on the return journey and, of course, got stuck again. I made some energetic endeavours to dig us out, but it was impossible; we had to wait a couple of hours until someone else came by to tow us. The weather had been steadily deteriorating ever since the landing, and that morning broke with a strong and extremely cold wind. Walcheren during the following days revealed itself as the coldest, windiest, and most inhospitable isle of my acquaintance.

When back in our parking ground, some of the Commandos, who had by this time cleared the dyke almost round to Flushing, were returning in small bodies to rest. With them long files of prisoners were now arriving, and a prison enclosure was set up on the hilltop close to the hospital tent. Our Commandos were weary and pretty hungry too. They had landed with a 24-hour pack in their kits, and since had had no rations of any kind. Those who had found German food had eaten, those who had not remained hungry. We helped a few of them out with a drink of tea when we made breakfast. Later in the morning there was some excitement; the war, apparently over in our sector, flared up again. We heard several loud explosions behind the dyke, which we took at the time for further mine detonations on the beach, and accordingly ate our breakfast without taking further notice. It was therefore a nasty jolt to our sense of security to discover that they were shells from a big gun mounted on rails, which owing to its mobility had hitherto escaped attention. More by luck than judgement, this little fusillade destroyed two more of the Engineers' Buffaloes parked on a beach nearer to the ill omened gap. However, after this one outburst of belated vindictiveness we had no more trouble from the gun in question, and these were the last casualties on our beaches. Domburg had also now fallen and resistance virtually ceased in the north of the island. In the afternoon we received a further assignment to help in moving the forces from the northern side over to our own sector. I saw nothing of the fighting here, which at first had been the most severe of the campaign.

There was by now a heavy sea surging through the gap, topped by big North Sea rollers, which made a further crossing of the minefield by the comparatively sheltered route we had used before too risky. We were obliged, therefore, to make the rough crossing, broadside to the waves immediately across the mouth of the gap. It was a difficult crossing in such a strong current, and the Buffaloes were hard put to make it. A fleet of Weazels, attempting to cross earlier in the day for supplies, had to give up the attempt. However, our luck held with the elements, as with the enemy. The dyke between Westkapelle and Domburg was much lower lying than where we had been operating, without sandhills, and had a road of sorts running along the top. Some of the enemy's biggest guns were here, their rounded cupolas split in two, and the guns themselves with burst barrels.

Here we picked up from a former German dugout a small party of Commandos and all the kit and stores belonging to their troop, including rations and cooking apparatus. There was not much of it, for the whole lot went into our Buffalo. Returning again to Westkapelle we fell again, inevitably, into a bomb crater. The usual futile endeavours to pull out merely exhausted our gallant craft still further; in this soft sand it was hopeless, and again operations were held up while another craft pulled us out. The sea had risen still further in the meantime, and crossing of the gap was now held to be too dangerous for Buffaloes to attempt, so this time we made our way inland and passed behind the minefield, a safe enough route, and now out of range of remaining enemy guns.

We took our cargo up to the same village, which was now becoming the base for further advances. On returning we had the mortification of getting stuck again, this time right on our own parking ground, and once again had to be towed out. Later in the day we had another unpleasant little job. Several Weazels, otherwise undamaged, were stuck off the beaches to the front of the gap where we had made the original landing. We had to crawl along the shore line to avoid the heavy sea among a tangle of barbed wire and general wreckage, and tow the Weazels back by the same route. We were very lucky to manage this job without either hitting a mine or having the craft turn turtle. We did become involved among the wire on two occasions, but the trusty old Buffalo managed this time to clear herself. It was just as well, for from this position we could not have been towed out.

Towards evening we started out in convoy along our now familiar trail, but the strain on our poor old craft was proving too much, for she seized this opportunity to break down. A violent banging sound from the side, upon inspection, resolved itself into one of the guide rollers for the track having been torn completely from its housing. We could not proceed further in this condition, and were instructed to remain where we were until fitters could be sent to us. As it turned out, no fitters came, and this was the end of active operations for my crew. We settled down and slept for the first time undisturbed for a whole night, even if fully clothed and at the ready. What bliss was the first night of sleep, under no matter what conditions, after these four nights of little or none at all! We stopped here waiting for instructions, until well into the next morning, meanwhile other Buffaloes, busy as bees, roared, crashed and jerked up and down the familiar track. Eventually a fitter did arrive, found he could not do the job on the spot, and received instructions to take us back to the nearest workshop. It was due to the fitter's inexpert guidance that the catastrophe happened. Just past the hospital we took a taped lane, which we thought led to the workshop, only unfortunately it led instead over an imperfectly cleared minefield.

We had not gone many yards when there was a dull muffled explosion somewhere underneath, the craft shuddered slightly and came to a stop. The forepart of the craft was blackened in a cloud of acrid-smelling smoke, and the fitter, who had been standing immediately over the explosion staggered back, dazed. There was no immediate sign of damage, but the engine did not start, and we felt instantly that, though everyone appeared to be unharmed, the craft was finished.

We dismounted gingerly and inspected the damage. The track was broken and a large hole had been blown in the belly of the craft, though the inside floor over the bilges was sound. She was not unrepairable, but under the limited local facilities it amounted to just that: she was finished. We took the dazed fitter to hospital, and our vehicle commander received instructions to strip the craft, which we then proceeded to do with heavy hearts.

I, an unmechanical man who normally hates mechanical things, felt a very real regret at the destruction of our gallant vehicle, which in so short a time had borne us safely over so many obstacles and through so much potential death. It approached my feeling for an ancient push bike which in happier times had borne me over tens of thousands of miles. This purely sentimental feeling, however, was soon mixed with more practical regrets as the full extent of our deprivation sank in. We had lost our vehicle: that meant that from the status of a useful unit of this expedition we had sunk to the level of unproductive cargo that someone else would have to carry. In addition, and more important really when you are stranded on a hostile flooded island swept by North Sea gales, we had lost our comparatively comfortable home and were cast out into the elements to manage as best we could. It was all very depressing.

As a foretaste of evil things to come, the wind, cold and strong on the previous day, had during the morning worked itself up to a pitch where loose sand from the top of the sandhills was blowing in stinging gusts: in fact on the landward side of the dyke a full scale desert-style sandstorm was developing, which became worse as the day wore on. I reflected, ironically, that this had happened on the 5th November, of all days. We, moreover, were by no means the only sufferers from this foul weather. For days seas were so high that LCTs were unable to land with much needed supplies.

Wind-buffeted and smothered in sand, we carried our sundry gear all the way from the fatal minefield to our old parking place. Carrying our most precious possession, the tarpaulin sheet, in such a gale was not an easy matter; but we had to do it, it was the only bulwark standing between us and the merciless elements.

We dropped our guns, wireless set and other tank equipment in a central material dump, and proceeded to erect ourselves as good a bivouac as we could contrive. It turned out to be not good enough.

We passed the day somewhat miserably sheltering from the howling hurricane, emerging only to cook when we had to. This was one of the many occasions when we thanked heaven for Compo rations, which heat in their tins without exposure to sandstorms. By evening the sandstorm was almost as unpleasant as the genuine desert variety, and the only way to escape, other than in our bivouac, was on the seaward side of the dyke where the wind was bitingly cold as I ever remember it. We settled for the night more in hope than in assurance of undisturbed repose. The wind howled and our sheet flapped and banged and, sure enough, about 1 am the catastrophe feared by all happened – it started to rain, in addition to the wind and sand; the combination was too much for our bivouac, and it collapsed on top of us. Some 20 minutes work in and out of the raging elements were required to make the thing something like weatherproof again. Another night I shall always look back upon with extreme disfavour, this one. To be as uncomfortable again I should have to wait for half a century to pass, and a tent pitched at 16,000 feet, close to the Mount Everest Base Camp.

The next day, with the weather somewhat improved but still pretty foul, was one of alarms and excursions, with neither us nor anyone else knowing what was to happen to us.

We started with the news that our craft was to be recovered, and consequently started to re-pack some of the stuff on board: then came news that we were leaving it and being evacuated; then again that our boys, having practically no craft left in a fit condition to operate, were all being returned to the mainland.

Meanwhile the campaign in general was moving rapidly to a close. Flushing, where 'A' Squadron had been operating, had fallen, and they had moved on to Middelburg, capital town in the centre of the island. Six 'A' Squadron Buffaloes, acting as tanks, had been among the first to enter this last centre of resistance on the island. Prisoners were now numerous in our own enclosure, and on this morning the weather moderated sufficiently to allow LCTs to bring in supplies and to take prisoners off. Something else I noticed, too, in passing the hospital; some 20 or 30 blanket-shrouded forms on stretchers, with just a pair of boots peeping out below. They had died of their wounds in spite of the devoted care of the medical staff. Inevitably, during the course of the war, one had seen many dead men; but I think of all I saw these close-stacked, still forms with limp feet protruding were the most tragic.

After taking down our bivouac hours before it was necessary and standing about in the cold waiting and packing our kit into one craft and having to unpack it again, eventually two of our dismounted crews (with heaven knows how much gear) were loaded into an 'A' Squadron craft which had been transferred to our sector. By arrangements similar to this all our lads were withdrawn from the area, leaving our wrecked or unserviceable Buffaloes behind.

We started in convoy towards evening along our familiar track, only this time following it right down to Flushing. It was intended that we should all reach there that evening and sleep in wrecked houses; and all but the craft I was riding in did so. Close to the town the track alongside the dyke became impassable, and the column had to diverge across the flooded fields. Our craft (it always seemed to happen to us) became caught up in the miles of wire lying about just as we were passing through a minefield. By the time we had ourselves disentangled, everyone else had disappeared from sight and no one knew the correct way to go.

We milled about for a while and eventually worked clear of the poles and wires, but found we were heading for the open gap where the sea rushed into the island adjoining Flushing. Clearly that was not the way, and we seemed to be right out of luck that evening. Reaching some semi-solid ground, we eventually found ourselves in a churchyard, flooded less deeply than the surrounding country. We were near to houses here, and thought we might be able to reach a road; but no! we got bellied again beautifully on top of a mound, from which nothing would induce the craft to shift.

It was now getting dark and starting to rain again. Everyone was as cold and miserable as possible, and we looked like having to spend another most uncomfortable night among the tombstones. We wirelessed for assistance, but were 'off net' and got no reply. We signalled by lamp, and did get a reply from somewhere but nothing came of it. To crown our misery, water started seeping in through the ramp joints and wet all the kit in the bottom of the craft.

Spirits hit an all-time low, as we shared the small stock of compo biscuits in an endeavour to generate a little warmth and cheer. At this point, fortunately, someone noticed that the tide was rising and urged the driver to try again to get us off. He did, and still nothing happened, but he kept on trying at intervals and after about an hour the lumbering craft at least pulled herself clear, to the accompaniment of vast sighs of relief. A short distance without further mishap brought us out on a tree-lined road in the outer residential part of the town.

Before proceeding further, I should mention that another of our squadron craft, making this same journey earlier on in the proceedings, had been swept out to sea through the gap in the dyke recently mentioned, and in endeavouring to make their way back their vehicle had been impaled through its belly on a 'dragon's tooth' anti-tank obstacle. Their craft was sinking slowly only a short distance from the shore, and a really thrilling sea rescue was effected, by the best swimmer aboard swimming ashore against a strong current and through heavy surf with a rope. Everyone was rescued, though the hero of the piece told me afterwards that it was a near thing with one fellow. It must have been an exciting little adventure, though I was mightily thankful, myself, that I had no occasion to swim in that icy water.

However, to return to my own adventures: chugging slowly up the road we were looking for any sort of habitable house in this completely inundated town. Presently we spotted a large building, evidently an institution of some kind. It was a modern building, undamaged except for a few broken windows, but with the ground floor, as with every other building on the island, under water. It was getting late, probably 9 or 10 o'clock by this time, and we therefore determined to try to get into this place for the night. It bore no outward sign of habitation.

Straight up the drive our Buffalo charged through about three feet of water, and pulled up immediately under the main entrance. One man climbed from the Buffalo to the porch roof with the intention of smashing a way in through a first floor window. He was in the very act of doing so, when a commotion was heard inside, revealing that the place was still occupied, and his hand was stayed just in time. The door was opened directly and our requirements of shelter for the night made known by degrees. We were welcomed like long lost relatives returned from the dead. The place turned out to be a modern and most beautifully equipped hospital, at the time occupied by a skeleton staff of a dozen or so, mostly women.

Kit came up through the landing window we had been about to force, and the porter carried each man of us in over the flooded ground floor on his back. We were taken to their kitchen, and forcibly set down, while they heated us water to wash in, made our tea, and cooked our supper for us. We were given a warm and comfortable rubber-floored room to sleep in, and they even laid down mattresses for us on the floor. So, instead of out in a leaking Buffalo in a desolate windswept churchyard in the rain, we spent our night sleeping in heavenly peace in this super-modern, centrally-heated paradise. Of all the rousing welcomes we received on the continent, I think this one, resulting from our surprise descent on this Flushing hospital in the middle of the night, was the warmest, most spontaneous and most appreciated.

Under a bright sky the pleasant and modern town of Flushing, known to me from happier days, wore many scars, and under its three or four feet of water looked very forlorn. Nearly every one of the neat, red, gabled houses, so widely spaced and well set out, had windows broken and roofs battered. Towards the older part of the town, parts of which were not under water, the streets were still filled with the rubble of bombardment, and in the old town and harbour area there was heavy damage. The people were just collecting themselves after the shock of battle.

It was sad indeed to see so ruined this lovely clean new town, a fine example of modern Dutch city building, and port of passage to countless Europe-bound tourists before the war. We found our surviving Buffaloes, mostly 'A' Squadron craft, were parked on a cleared bomb site in the old town close to the harbour, and we waited around these for the rest of the day. A sizeable crowd of friendly local inhabitants soon collected. Our lads gave them German cigarettes they had found, and they gave us in return the last of their apple crop. Little groups of bilingual conversations were going on all over the squares. Those who found conversation too difficult just watched and smiled.

While we were waiting, our Divisional Commander came round to see us, and spent some time talking to the lads. One of the survivors from the first craft to catch fire after the landing, with a little round German sailor hat perched on his head, gave the General a graphic account, with actions, of the loss of his craft. All present including the Dutch spectators, were suitably entertained.

Long columns of the scruffiest, most miserable and dejected looking German prisoners passed dockwards for embarkation to the mainland. To look at these battered physical wrecks (they looked what they were, a division of stomach sufferers) it seemed incredible that they could really have been responsible for the hot reception we had received in the initial stages. The answer, of course, is that a physical wreck can fight as well in modern fixed defences as anyone else. In the late afternoon we were informed of the next step. All men of our battalion were being taken off, and all vehicles were being left behind to make up the losses of the Engineers, who were staying behind to finish the job. It had by this time started to rain again and there was a high sea running. We had a pretty rough crossing in an LCA (landing assault craft) over the Scheldt to Breskens, where we arrived wet, and frozen to the marrow.

We were housed in a partially wrecked dockside warehouse, the walls full of shellholes through which the wind howled, and the roof full of leaks through which the rained dripped, making pools on the floor. However, there was fuel there and we were able to get two roaring great fires going which improved matters vastly. After some trial and error we also found dry spots for everybody to sleep. That night and the next day we spent in this somewhat cheerless abode. Breskens was, I think, the most completely destroyed town in Holland, in almost as parlous a state as some of the rubble piles that once were towns in Normandy. I doubt if it contained an undamaged building.

For the next night we were found a little paper-and-matchwood workman's house, with undamaged lower storey, a fire and fuel. We had to wade over much water to get in and out, but managed to sleep above water level.

The next morning our lorries arrived to carry us back to our unit and that, for us, was the end of this little adventure.

The epic of Walcheren? Yes, I think from what I saw that it merits that title.

10
We hang out our washing on the Siegfried Line

After Walcheren we entered a world of 'water, water everywhere'; for it seemed the whole border area between Belgium, Holland and Germany was one vast flood in which it was impossible for anything except our amphibious vehicles to operate. Just where all the water came from I never discovered, but presumably from flooding of the many rivers in the area. With all normal landmarks hidden by the floods, we were never even sure which country we were operating in. The troops were paid in token paper money valid only for a particular country; but in any case in the middle of a flood there was nothing to buy even if war-torn western Europe had anything to sell. In Holland, at least, they had nothing, for the unfortunate Dutch, ground under the iron heel of the infamous Nazi Gauleiter, Seyss Inquart, suffered more than any other western European nation. In Holland there was literally noting to eat. Neighbouring Belgium undoubtedly did much better under a less vicious Gauleiter.

An oddity of this period was one occasion when members of our bemused Battalion asked the locals which country we were in, 'Holland, Belgium or where?' to be met by the disconcerting reply, 'We are Limburgers.'

We were in the narrow finger of territory, the Dutch province of Limburg, which stretches down between Belgium and Germany. Evidently, the Limburgers, if no one else, regarded themselves as an independent nation, no matter what the map might say.

Before we entered the main flooded area, when there was still high ground surrounding, we performed our first river crossing operation, ferrying assault infantry, 6 pounder guns and Bren carriers over the Wessem Canal, near the small town of Venlo. This episode sticks in my mind mainly because it was during this that B Squadron sustained its only fatal casualties – precisely two of them. Apparently, preliminary preparation had failed to dispose of one German self-propelled gun, and it was an unpleasant surprise to have this open up on us. Since Walcheren we had met with no opposition, and everyone was surprised and shocked when one of our corporals, and one junior officer, were killed. By incredible chance the latter was the son of a family who lived almost opposite my own in Sutton Coldfield, Warwickshire. I was particularly sorry about the latter, for he, also, had appeared with myself in a revue the Squadron had produced while we were in the Palestine desert. Yes, we even went in for amateur theatricals during our period of 'phoney' war.

So we entered the barren wastes of water, mainly some six or eight feet deep, which covered the whole frontier area. We could not tell, for there were no obvious landmarks, exactly where the frontier lay, though it was marked, very effectively, by Germany's ultimate defence line, the Siegfried Line, giving origin to the wartime song, 'We'll hang out our washing on the Siegfried Line'.

But the Siegfried Line in our sector was well under water, and we found it only when our Buffalo came to a sudden, grinding halt with a great steel spike stuck through its floor. The Siegfried Line, we presumed, borrowing the famous words of when Stanley met Livingstone. We were about as firmly stuck as anyone could be, and there was not a thing we could do about it. There was no option but to send out a distress wireless signal and wait for the Royal Engineers to send one of their special vehicles to lift us off.

So what did we do? The British Army has never been accused of failing to make the best of the most impossible situations. All the crew inevitably had very dirty socks by this time, so we washed them in the flood water and hung them out to dry on the wireless aerial. So we literally 'hung out our washing on the Siegfried Line'. Quite an achievement and surely absolutely unique!

Being lifted off the spike is something which should have stuck in my memory, but did not. Anyway, it evidently happened, for my next memory is of our Buffalo making its way into the war-torn town of Kleve, known historically as capital of the petty German state from which emerged Anne of Cleves, the unattractive fourth wife of King Henry VIII, who was disposed of by divorce. When we entered Kleve there was not much of it left. There was a ruined cathedral and, of course, everything was under water. The trivial incident that sticks in my mind was of Captain Allen, then in charge of my troop, who had got his trousers soaked, taking possession of the house of the former Mayor, and borrowing one of the latter's pairs of dry trousers. As I remember, the town had been completely evacuated, for there did not seem to be any intact building remaining.

Eventually we emerged on to the higher ground of the Hochwald Forest, leading to the Rhine, Germany's historic barrier and our really important river crossing. So we concluded our wettest episode, and the most complete contrast to the sands of the Palestine desert.

11
The Rhine – we storm the moat of the robber baron's castle

The great day approached. We were about to force Germany's last great national barrier, the Rhine.

The significance of this event weighed heavily upon one's conscience, for everyone along the great battle front realised that upon the result of this enterprise depended the early end of the war in Europe. Not only that, but also release from their bondage of the war-weary men who longed to go home and live the lives of civilised people once again.

This, after the landings in Normandy, would be the most massive operation ever planned by the British Army, one of the most complicated co-ordinations of supply and variety of arms the world had ever seen. For weeks the British armies had been preparing under a 60-mile-long smokescreen. The enemy, of course, knew we were coming. He knew that it would probably be in this sector; but we sincerely hoped that he did not know at precisely what point, or points, along this long front we should attack. On this hope we based our confidence, together with the belief that he would not have sufficient men or material to cover adequately the whole possible front.

We had travelled up by tank transporter from Belgium, prepared and equipped as never before for any eventuality. Our Buffaloes had all been thoroughly overhauled, and this time we felt that they would be in condition to stand up to the strain ahead of them. We hoped so, for we knew that upon us and our kindred units success of the entire operation depended more than upon anyone else whatsoever. Our task was to make the assault crossing of the river, and then to keep on ferrying across reinforcements and material until such time as sufficient bridges could be built to carry all the necessary traffic. Until the bridges were built, we were the bridges, and we had to keep going until then.

Upon arrival, we parked up in a most delightful little glade in the Hochwald forest, a short distance from Xanten. Here we set about the usual business of camouflaging our vehicles and covering up our track marks and any other signs that might give away our presence to enemy air-spotters; that is, in the unlikely event of the latter daring to appear. We lived for three days among the shady depths of this wood, lying sunbathing under our camouflage nets, listening to the birds, having a wash-down or some such little personal job.

There was little to do, for all preparation of our vehicles had already been carried out. We walked in the pinewoods, so thick and dark that the sunlight hardly penetrated their canopy. We listened to briefing lectures giving the last minute details of the operation to come, and we just sat and luxuriated in the glorious, unseasonable sunshine, drinking in the beauty of this incredible spring. If ever there was a perfect prelude to a mortal conflict, this was one. Whether for just gazing at the blue sky or for drawing from its brightness assurance of success for our enterprise, conditions were alike ideally designed.

This process, which I might describe as psychological preparation for battle, is not without its importance. Nothing is more worrying than to be rushed into these things without time to work up the nervous tension. Once the issue is joined, concentration on what he is doing will keep each man's mind free from fear; but in the period of waiting that always precedes an attack, when his stomach is a fluttering void and the future looms before him as an unknown quantity, it is the mood of almost spiritual exaltation he works up beforehand that enables him to weather the period of stress.

Preparation for battle might almost be compared to the training of an athlete for a race. He must be trained for just the right period with work and rest in proper proportion; if he is overtrained he goes stale. This period before the Rhine crossing was just of the correct duration to enable one to work up the right mood.

If the wait is too long, and the emotional peak is passed, a reaction of intense nervous irritation, most damaging to morale, is liable to follow. In particular, to have an operation postponed several times is, nervously, the most exhausting thing possible; upon each successive occasion it becomes more difficult to work up the right nervous tension.

We had a few preparatory jobs to do while in the wood, in connection with preparing the ground over which we were to operate, and we went up by lorry one morning to a field closely approaching the great river. Here a cottage was selected, and cleared up for the purpose, to serve as our Squadron Headquarters for the operation. It was situated immediately behind the second dyke, or bund, to use the correct German term, which bounds the west bank of the Rhine. Most of the lower reaches of major German rivers have these bunds to prevent flooding of the adjacent country, and on the west bank the Rhine had two. The main bund, about 15 feet high on the river side, was, at the time, some 50 feet back from the water's edge. About a quarter of a mile of level field separated this from the smaller bund behind which we made our headquarters.

In front of Squadron HQ were marked out, with poles and white tape, parallel lanes for the various troops of Buffaloes to park their vehicles. Adjoining were further lanes for the various services, the fitters, the recovery section, and other technical people so necessary to our successful operation. Behind was the petrol and oil dump, situated in a former German trench and covered by camouflage nets. Long taped lanes, with green lamps hanging on poles at regular intervals, were laid out from our rear assembly area in the wood to the point on the bund immediately opposite to the spot where we were to enter the water. Where the route crossed the secondary bund, a gap was cleared through it by that most essential of modern instruments of war, the bulldozer.

The point at which we were to leave the water after the first assault was also to be marked by lights, and from here a further taped route led back from the bund to the assembly area, and Squadron HQ adjoining. On the river side of the small bund was the loading area, where we were to pick up the vehicles to be taken across when we started ferrying. We relied upon the high bund, combined with the smokescreen, to shield all these preparations from the enemy's eyes.

This country bordering the Rhine, after emerging from the Hochwald forest, was open, flat and rather featureless. It consisted of large grazing fields, broken only by ditches and the high bunds. There were a few smallish trees and straggly hedges, but it was mainly open ground and ideal for manoeuvre. A mile or so on our right flank lay the almost obliterated little town of Xanten, with only its church tower rising from the rubble.

One unusual feature of the landscape was the system of long German trenches snaking across the open fields, endless zigzag affairs like the trenches of the last war, and never before seen in this one; a symbol of the last desperate stand the enemy made on our side of the river a few weeks before. Other signs were not wanting either; notably large numbers of black and white Friesian cattle, some of them badly mutilated, lying about in the fields.

In the course of several briefings we gradually built up a comprehensive picture of what was about to happen. In brief, it was this. The Canadians were to make a diversion in front of Arnhem earlier on, in the hope that the enemy would be deluded into believing that this was the point of attack. Meanwhile the Second Army was attacking on a two-corps front some 10 miles long between the towns of Rees in the north and Wesel in the south. Three main crossings were being made, all principally by means of Buffaloes; by 30th Corps at Rees with the 51st Highland Division, by 12th Corps at Xanten spearheaded by the 15th Scottish Division. Further south again the American 9th Army was launching a proportionate, and simultaneous attack of its own.

Our own battalion was attacking at separate points in two squadrons, B and C Squadrons, A Squadron this time being in reserve and serving to bring the other two up to strength. My own Troop constituted the first wave of B Squadron's attack, the Troop, again, being in two waves of three vehicles each. We were scheduled to enter the water at 2 am, the northern attack at Rees being earlier on the same evening at 9 pm.

After the third glorious day in the wood we heard that today was to be the eve of the attack. All was prepared, and a great silence of expectancy settled over the waiting thousands. Indeed, looking about, this was the most remarkable aspect of the whole affair: the silence and lack of disturbance of the rural peace caused by these vast preparations. Hidden somewhere in this small area were tens of thousands of men, thousands of guns, tanks and transport vehicles, and the most colossal accumulation of ammunition ever seen. The entire strength of the 2nd Army was here, each unit in its appointed order and place, waiting for us to set the ball rolling. Of all this vast concourse, apart from an occasional lorry or dispatch rider, or perhaps a small group of pioneers digging a hole for something or other, there was not a thing to be seen. All was smooth, unruffled, undisturbed; just a chunk of rural Germany apparently differing in no way from other parts. Yet behind all this our Army crouched, disturbing the surface of the countryside no more than a tiger disturbs the jungle underbrush.

Of all the vast numbers of guns being moved into position we actually saw no more than one battery of 5·5 inch medium artillery which appeared to be in our wood. Yet every artillery piece the 2nd Army possessed was somewhere in this area. Each unit, for all it could see to the contrary, might have been attacking all by itself.

Round about mid-afternoon we heard the first few ranging shots of the massive artillery barrage that continued unbroken for the whole of this night, the next day, and part of the next. From now until we crossed the river the barrage rose in crescendo until the night was filled with its continuous, rolling thunder. This was indeed an epoch-making show; everything about it was the biggest ever.

It was said after the Spanish Armada that 'God blew with his wind and they were scattered'. This time it might be said with equal purpose that He shone with His sun to similar effect. The sun sank from a cloudless blue sky, giving the promise of yet more perfect weather for the all-important tomorrow.

As dusk fell, we cleared away our camouflage, warmed up engines, loaded guns and pulled out into the roadway ready for loading up. Dark files of infantry, loaded with the usual mountains of equipment, appeared apparently from nowhere, and loaded themselves on to our waiting craft. We hung about until around 11 pm before moving off, this allowing a full hour to cover possible mishaps over the time scheduled to be taken to reach the river at the specified hour – 2 am. This had to be timed exactly, as the barrage was arranged to lift off the landing beaches precisely at the moment we were to enter the water. An error on either side here could have had disastrous consequences.

The moon rose as we moved, making our surroundings as clearly visible as in daylight. Behind, in the direction from which we had come, lines of white flashes ran up and down the horizon, now darting backward and forward, now merging into a solid wall of flame. Such is the odd effect of the delay in the sound of firing reaching the ears, that the background of rolling thunder appeared to have no connection with the flashes.

Overhead was a noise of shells hurtling through the air; a roaring sound with big ones, a higher, whining sound with smaller. Endless streams of tracer shells, mostly Bofors, came over in graceful arcs almost like water out of a hosepipe. The bounds of each attack were marked by two such streams of tracers which kept going incessantly. Flashes and explosions on the enemy's side, punctuated by coloured flares, helped to make the world's finest firework display.

I amused myself, during our slow progress broken by many stops, by listening to the sometimes very funny snatches of conversation coming over the wireless. The main topic of conversation related to one craft that had broken down. The squadron commander lost touch with it, and endless messages passed in an endeavour to re-establish contact. There was also some argument with the officer in charge at the crossing point of the final bund, who had arrived at his destination too early. He reported enemy shellfire at that point.

We were getting near now; we passed through the gap bulldozed in the first bund. At this point we opened out from our line-ahead formation into line abreast, fanning out to our correct intervals apart as we did so. Now the tall final bund loomed ahead. I shut my operator's hatch, and retired inside.

Our Buffalo reared, pointing its nose to the sky, regained the horizontal with a terrific jerk, then plunged seemingly into the bottomless pit as we rushed down the opposite slope of the bund. As it did so, I drew in my breath, bracing myself to receive the expected tornado of shells – but nothing happened.

We charged full speed for the water, the Buffalo dropped its nose again, and entered with its usual almighty splash. Now we were running smoothly on the water – and still nothing happened. I looked through my periscope and could see nothing in particular but grey water. Could it actually be that we were going to get away with this? I let out my breath again and opened up the hatch.

Nothing was to be seen on the other side – absolutely nothing but the other bank appearing as a grey blur, and the broad river, silvery and mysterious in the moonlight, covered by a slight mist. Its surface was smooth, hardly rippled and we could feel hardly any current. It seemed not nearly so wide as one's imagination had pictured it to be.

Our driver shouted to the commander over the inter-com for a check of direction, and I could pick out without difficulty the little bay formed by two of the groins, or small shingle breakwaters, with which the banks were lined. Our gunner fired a couple of rounds from the ·50 Browning machine gun, after which the gun jammed. It did not matter, for there was nothing to fire at anyway. Not a sign of life was to be seen on the far bank; it might as well have been the surface of the moon.

We passed into the little bay; our 400-yard crossing had taken only a matter of minutes. The three Buffaloes touched down almost together, my own just slightly ahead. We ran our nose ashore on a perfect sandy beach, unimpeded by any steep bank, and our infantry jumped smartly over the front. We backed out into the river again, turned left and followed our two consorts downstream and out of the water by the landing light.

It was over, and we were still here and all in one piece. Not only had no opposition been met on this, which should have been one of the most dangerous operations of the whole war, but from first to last not a shot had been fired at us. Still almost unbelieving, we bowled along the return route to the assembly area. As we went, I picked up wireless messages from each of the succeeding Buffalo troops reporting that they had landed safely. None of them had any trouble, though there was a certain amount of Spandau fire later on, causing most of the craft to fire back while crossing.

The first phase had been completed with clockwork precision; the great river had been crossed by our assault infantry. Now started the next phase, reinforcement of the assault troops on a scale sufficient to maintain the new bridgehead until bridges were built to take over the main forces. Again, it depended on us.

We reached the previously prepared concentration area and parked up in our appointed troop lane. As instructed, we dug slit trenches in case the enemy should wax aggressive, but there was no occasion to use them. Vehicles trickled back one by one until all were in. We stood by, but nothing else happened before dawn, when we repaired to the Squadron HQ for breakfast and to talk over the momentous events of the night.

There is always something vaguely unreal about these night attacks viewed from about 7 am of the morning after, when the effects of a sleepless night and the nervous tension have had time to wear off. The night with its fantastic shadowy happenings, its alarms and uncertainties, might never have been at all. It belonged more to the world of nightmare than to the everyday world that we know, and particularly upon such a fair morning as this was. Gone were all the terrors of darkness and the unknown; even the far bank was now friendly and welcoming territory instead of the deadly menace it was the night before. Except for the booming of artillery, not so concentrated or continuous now, the events of the night might have been a figment of the imagination.

After breakfast we crossed the bund into the loading area, where already a long line of loaded Bren Carriers awaited us. We loaded one, and started on the first of many round trips made that day. This time we did not need to climb the bund, as a gap had already been bulldozed through it.

Again we dived into the river, looking so different in the early morning haze, and of even lesser proportions than it had appeared by night. The far bank, broken at regular intervals by groins, consisted of flat, almost treeless grazing fields sloping up gently from the sandy beach. Apparently the east bank is not liable to flood, as it differs chiefly from the western in possessing no bund. Not a specially exciting stretch of the historic river; still it appeared pleasant to us on this morning, with clear water and our spray sparkling in the sun.

Our little beach showed remarkably little sign of activity, considering the numbers who had landed upon it. A defence platoon in slit trenches was taking it easy; there was a beach control NCO directing the Buffaloes in landing, and another superintending their unloading. The flag planted on the beach by my Troop Commander to mark the first landing was still there, and that was about all.

The river was quite full. Once we commenced ferrying, there were always some ten or a dozen Buffaloes in the water at once. Little outboard-motor assault boats dashing about, and two or three naval craft stranded on a sandbank, made the place look more like Henley Regatta than Germany's very own historic western rampart. Also stuck on a sandbank were three or four of our special water-proofed amphibious tanks, of which a battalion had crossed at first light. Several Buffaloes were trying to pull these out, and all but two were floated successfully. These two remained there for the rest of the operation, their stranded crews gazing forlornly out of the top at us as we worked.

We returned by the same circle route we had used during the night, checked in at Squadron HQ, and made the same round again. Throughout the day we continued to follow the same routine, except that about midday the loading area was moved forward into the large field between the two bunds, where there was more room for manoeuvre.

Towards ten o'clock we started to glance skywards into the thick morning haze, a promise of sweltering heat to come: this, amazingly enough, on the morning of 24th March. We were looking for the next stage in the operation, the landing by 18th Airborne Corps in the enemy's rear areas due at about this time. Sure enough, a solid wedge-shaped formation of about twenty Dakota transport planes loomed out of the haze ahead, as yet indistinct, but unmistakable. They were flying low, probably not more than 1,000 feet up.

Gradually the air filled with a mighty droning that almost drowned the sound of our own noisy engines, and formation after formation of Dakotas emerged from the mist and disappeared again into it; the first wave of the airborne army, carrying the paratroops. The British 6th Airborne passed slightly to the north of us; the American division directly overhead.

After half an hour the haze cleared, leaving cloudless blue sky, and we could see better what was happening. Surely never before did anyone receive such an impression of dynamic, all-pervading power. I had seen many of the biggest bomber raids, but never was there anything to compare with this spectacle; possibly there never will be again. Natural phenomena aside, it was about the most terrific thing this old earth had yet seen; the most overwhelming display of purely man-made might ever staged. Small wonder that the enemy did not put up much of a fight; it was a sight calculated to make us feel as invincible as a legion of angels, and to fill them with fear: a sight to make the courage of the most desperate last-ditch defenders ooze out through their boots. The moral effect on the enemy must have been like that on a boxer in the ring, battered almost to a standstill already, being hit suddenly over the head with a steam hammer.

Like a horde of giant locusts they stretched in unbroken column over the sky behind us, sometimes in large formations of 50 or 60 aircraft, sometimes in smaller groups of 20 odd but always flying tightly packed, wing-tip to wing-tip. Towards the horizon, with the lengthening perspective, the swarm seemed to thicken into a solid black mass, blotting out the sky. Wave after wave they came, almost without a break. It seemed they would never stop; as if there never was a time when the air was not full of droning monsters. For some five hours, from ten in the morning until three in the afternoon they came unendingly, with only one short break between the first wave of parachutists and the second wave of gliders.

Across the river we could now see the pattern of attack. The separate columns of the two divisions had landing points some distance apart. We saw clearly the showers of gleaming white parachutes, each with its tiny human atom swinging like a pendulum below, being spilled from the belly of each monster. We saw, too, the puffs of anti-aircraft shells turning this section of the sky into a hazy mass of smoke. We saw the tight formations breaking up before the wall of fire, and edging round the smoke cloud trying to find a clear way on to their objective. We saw more than one Dakota gliding rapidly earthwards with a column of black smoke pouring from its tail.

Those planes that came through unscathed returned singly by the same route; not a few of the less fortunate circled round, tongues of flame licking at them, looking for any spot to crash-land. I saw two explode in the air and several more dive headlong to earth, black smoke spiralling up from where they landed.

Mixed with the Dakotas were formations of Liberator bombers, dropping supplies by coloured parachute. One returned overhead with three of its four engines burning, long trails of fire streaming out behind. It kept steadily on its course, apparently unembarrassed by what looked from the ground to be a hopeless situation.

One burning Dakota jettisoned its parachutists immediately over our heads from a low level, and we had a grandstand view of an actual landing. They spilled from the plane in rapid succession, just like a row of peas being shelled from a pod. The parachutes opened immediately, and by the time each had swung back and forth two or three times he was down. The man landed with a jerk, while the parachute collapsed slowly and gracefully like a wilting flower shedding its petals. They all landed in quite a small area in the next field to our own; the men disentangled themselves in an incredibly short time and ran to rally in a bunch. Some of our people took charge of them.

After another half hour or so of this stiff opposition, the paratroops had evidently accounted for the enemy guns, for the sky cleared again and formations could be seen opening out into single line and circling, each unloading its cargo in perfect order. From this moment there could be no doubt of the operation's success. At last the first wave was over; there was a short interval and then came the gliders. One Dakota towing two gliders, forming a triangle of three; triangles of three seeming to stretch round the earth. Over the objective each apex plane circled and returned while the two gliders dipped and drifted to earth. Not till late afternoon did the terrific spectacle end with waves of five Liberators flying in line, carrying the bulk of the supplies. They passed over only a few hundred feet high with shattering roar, casting monstrous shadows on the ground.

While the air armada was passing over our heads, we on the river bank were not idle. On the loading field long columns of Bren Carriers, amphibian Weazels, 6 pounder anti-tank guns and Jeeps lined up waiting their turn; facing them in a row with ramps dropped ready for loading, our Buffaloes formed up. With clockwork regularity, and hardly a pause between runs, the same routine took place.

Pull into position, drop the ramp, load the vehicle, wind up the ramp and into the river; out the other side to the unloading spot indicated by the beachmaster, ramp down, vehicle off, ramp up, and back again for another; over and over and over again. One of our consorts counted 36 round trips that day; many must have done even more.

It was pleasant to notice the first aid post as we passed it on each run, completely empty with the staff lounging outside. My craft carried back only two wounded, German infantrymen, throughout the day. On the landing beach I saw the digging of two British graves. One of the dead was having his possessions removed; shrapnel in the chest had killed him. These two were the only British dead on this beach; a measure of our overwhelming success.

Towards midday we had our first break, one man at a time from each crew dropping out for an hour for a rest. I could not sleep during my hour off; I just lay and basked in the sun, watching the endless procession of aircraft.

During one lull I had a look round the beach. There was remarkably little evidence to be seen on the ground of the tremendous barrage; not nearly so many shell holes as one would expect. This was due to the altering technique of artillery barrages, which in this campaign contained a high proportion of airburst shells; the idea being rather to force the enemy to keep all heads down while our attack was on, and to deprive him of the advantage of ground cover, rather than to blast him out of the ground. The air-burst shell, not wasting its energy on the unresponsive ground, was much more deadly in its effect, and paid dividends in saved lives.

By evening the accumulation of vehicles had been completely disposed of, and we were able to deal with such few as came during the night by having one Troop on duty at a time, while the remainder slept. The blessed relief of those few hours sleep, if still fully dressed and ready for emergency!

There was no definite news as yet of the progress of the battle, but it is usually possible to tell from the nature of the firing how things are going. Artillery fire had been only desultory throughout the day, with occasional bursts of ferocity. While first thing in the morning the slow, rattling bursts of Bren and answering bursts of Spandau, so rapid that individual shots cannot be distinguished, were near and insistent, by evening they were almost out of earshot. We heard that our forces were some eight miles in, and that a junction had been effected between them and the airborne troops.

Another sure indication we had learned to know of the progress of battle was the moving up of our artillery, which we saw taking place this evening. The 25 pounders were moved up close to the river, and opening again concentrated fire on the enemy's main centres of resistance around Emmerich, and in the small pocket formed at Rees, to the north of us; they kept up a deafening clatter all night.

During the one trip we made in the night the river was smoother, softer, more ethereal than before. There is something about this river. Other rivers are longer, wider, swifter, but none holds the same magic as this stream of floating legend, fable and history. At dead of night among all the pandemonium of modern war, the mysterious spirit of the ancient river was still dominant. Hitler was right here; the Rhine *is* German, it is the very core and essence of the spirit of Germanism.

In some mystical way, I believe that the river was so symbolic to the enemy that their minds were already conquered by our action in crossing it. If the spirits of the gods and heroes could not preserve inviolate their own dwelling place, of what use was it for mere man to struggle further? This was the moment of final climax to the war in the west; the moment when Germany's strength ebbed out of her as did that of Samson under the shearing of his locks, and the will to fight left her.

The next morning dawned bright and clear, and at an early hour another vast concourse of vehicles had assembled, awaiting our services. Most of the British vehicles had now been disposed of, and during this second day we were dealing mainly with the transport of the American airborne division. Jeeps and trailers by the hundreds: it seemed impossible that there could be so many Jeeps in the world. However, this went off even quicker than the previous day's operations, as the Jeeps were easy to load.

Of course, this was not a matter one could have discussed at the time, but there was a strong rumour going that we ought never to have had to handle the American transport; that this ought to have been dropped directly by air on the battle front. The rumour was that the Americans had made a navigational error and dropped their loads over the wrong river, mistaking the Maas for the Rhine. As a result, later, of seeing with my own eyes an example of American bombing of a wrong target, I would not be surprised if this rumour were true. Also, a new gap had been made in the bund whereby we might return directly to the loading area by the same route that we went out, instead of following the circuit route of the original attack. As C Squadron had now finished on their beach they came to help us, and the river became one surging mass of Buffaloes; we were hard put to it to avoid collisions.

By this time both loading area and landing beach had become much churned up and muddy from the water discharged from the Buffaloes' bilges. It was lucky that there was sufficient heat to dry up the ground almost as quickly as we wet it. There can be little doubt that just one shower of rain would have been enough to make loading difficult or impossible, and possibly to wreck the whole operation. Such was the measure of good fortune, or Divine dispensation, that attended our efforts.

During the morning we could see downsteam from us a Class 40 bridge, the type capable of taking tanks and heavy lorries, making excellent progress. By midday the 400-yard-wide river had been spanned, and the first traffic could be seen crossing. Already the end of our job was in sight, as was that of the powered rafts, which during the two days had ferried across an appreciable amount of armour and heavy equipment.

By afternoon we had disposed of the Americans and their miles of Jeeps, and by evening a further collection of our own Weazels and 6 pounders. This was the main part of the job done. During the night the Guards Armoured Division crossed by the new bridge, and so did the 25 pounders in this sector. There were rumours of our advanced units being 20 miles in, and the certainty of their being ten or twelve miles deep from the fact of the artillery having been moved up. The issue was now beyond doubt; the bridgehead was secure and the river line broken. Those two days had converted a possible impasse into a certain victory.

We took a few more vehicles next morning to ease the strain on the several bridges now working, then parked up close to the inner bund. The crossing operation began on the night of 23rd-24th March, being virtually completed on the morning of the 26th.

We parked in a field full of dead cattle, the inevitable innocent victims of war, swollen and bloated into fantastic shapes as if they were rubber blow-up toys. A number of these were not battle casualties, but had died of milk fever from there being no one available to milk them. The Squadron Weazel dragged them on a tow-rope to a central dump, making a huge pile of dozens of dead cattle.

During the next three days we put our Buffaloes in order again, and caught up on our sleep. On the 26th the Squadron had the honour of transporting the Prime Minister and his party over the river in one of our Buffaloes when he visited this sector; a fitting climax to the occasion.

During the aftermath of the great event the main interest was at night. In daylight the Luftwaffe did not dare to show themselves, but no sooner had the last patrol of Spitfires returned in the failing light with their navigation lights burning, than the former masters of the skies made several attempts to get at our bridges. The main bridge at Wesel had a balloon barrage to protect it, and so red did the sky become with streams of tracer shell that the silver balloons caught the light and reflected a glow, appearing like a great fire among the clouds. There were three Bofors guns in our field, a battery of 3·7 just below, and the heavy artillery still pounding away at the obstinate centre of resistance around Emmerich. All these made a grand firework display, and the noise had by now become so familiar that something seemed to be missing when it ceased. It becomes like sleeping in a room with a loudly ticking clock; you cannot sleep without it.

It was one of our local Bofors that caused the Squadron's only casualties on the operation. Firing at a diving plane, it hit a tree bordering the field, and shrapnel from the burst caused minor injuries to three of our lads bivouacking opposite.

After the third day here the heavy artillery departed over the river, and on the fifth, when we were withdrawn into Holland, a bulldozer had filled up the breaches in the bund, all sight and sound of battle had departed, and there might never have been any war on the banks of the Rhine.

The British armies were now deep into the heart of Germany, and the ancient river flowed on undisturbed, as if there had never been a fantastic ferry service churning its waters, and as if the greatest air fleet ever seen had never blotted out the sky above it. Yet, in spite of the river's unconcern this flat and uninteresting stretch had seen some amazing things. The four Buffalo regiments operating had made between them nearly 4,000 trips across its legendary waters, and of over 400 craft employed had lost only nine.

12
Over the plain and far away

Our Rhine crossing was absolutely decisive and, as we expected, once strong British forces were across the river the war was effectually over.

So we crossed the Rhine once more, this time via one of the Bailey Bridges, and mounted our Buffaloes on tank transporters for the road journey to our last objective, the river Elbe.

A finer sightseeing platform than a Buffalo on a tank transporter I cannot imagine, and it seemed a pity that the North German plain does not offer much interesting scenery. I remember passing through one historic German town, Celle; otherwise there was nothing much of interest but a string of farmhouses, all of which seemed to be flying at least three white flags – just to make sure. I wonder whether we British would have been quite so abject in defeat had the war gone the other way, as it so easily might have done?

We duly passed right through Luneburg Heath, the German Army's traditional training ground and the equivalent of Salisbury Plain. We finished up at Lauenburg, right on the western bank of the Elbe, there ending our sightseeing tour of the north German plain and preparing for our last river crossing.

Crossing the Elbe by Buffalo was about as unlike as possible to what crossing the Rhine had been. There was no opposition at all; it was just a transport job. For the very last thing the remnants of the German Army on the far side of the river wanted was to antagonise the British, to whom they were only too ready to surrender. What they wanted above everything was to avoid falling into the hands of the Russians, knowing full well that they would receive no more mercy from the latter than they had meted out to Russians in the days of their early triumphs back in 1941.

Units we had by-passed were surrendering in droves. They were just relieved of their weapons and directed to the nearest prisoner-of-war cage. They were not even provided with an escort. By this stage of the war, if not before, most of our men were conscious that we were not fighting *Germans*, anyway, we were, most of us, just fighting Nazis, and all that they stood for.

We did not know it at the time, but several of our arch enemies perished at around this time, mostly by their own hands. Both Himmler and Goebbels died of self-inflicted poison, the former after he had been officially arrested. A particular British aversion, the traitor, 'Lord Haw Haw', who made the Nazis' broadcasts to the British people during the war, gave himself up voluntarily and, to everyone's satisfaction, was one of the few war criminals actually to be hanged. Goering was brought to trial at Nuremburg, but managed to swallow poison during the trial. Hitler, himself, of course also died of poison in his bunker in Berlin, together with his newly-married wife, Eva Braun. It appears he might have escaped to south Germany if he had acted in time, but chose not to, preferring a 'Gotterdammerung' end.

The final defence of Berlin was a pretty desperate affair, for perhaps the most poignant war memorial I have seen was the Russian war memorial in East Berlin. It is a simple conical mound surmounted by the figure of a Russian soldier. It commemorates the 20,000 Russians killed in the final assault on Berlin, after the war had officially ended. When I visited Berlin in the 1970s, there was no memorial to the Germans killed in the same battle.

But, back at the Elbe, we made another copy-book crossing, just as if it had been opposed, and bridges were rapidly constructed to take advance forces across the river. On the far side was a sight indeed for the gods: what remained of the German army in that sector neatly drawn up and wearing their best uniforms, carrying their suitcases – but without weapons. They were just waiting to be directed to the safety of the British prisoner-of-war cages – anything to avoid falling into the hands of the Russians, who, a little further south, met up with the American advance guard.

No sooner had the German army units crossed the Elbe, than the host of released allied prisoners-of-war, conscripted foreign workers for the German war effort or just displaced persons, poured in droves over the bridges, carrying whatever goods and chattels they could. This was one occasion when I really regretted not being able to take photographs in war conditions.

The atmosphere of an historic moment was caught when our chaps, by then with nothing to do, just crowded around our ends of the bridges and watched in wonder. One of them called out to one small, round-shouldered, clerical-looking type pushing an enormous wheelbarrow piled high with all the useful domestic junk he could find, 'It's a long way to Tipperary, mate.' To which the unfortunate, but heroic little man replied, 'It's a long way to Amsterdam,' a mere matter of some 300 miles on the map. I hope he made it, but hardly, I think, with his barrow-full of junk.

After this, everything was anti-climax, degenerating into farce. We had more sightseeing trips organised, first to the ruined city of Hamburg and if ever there was a completely ruined city, it was Hamburg early in 1945. There did not seem to be a single building standing from our viewpoint. Indeed I could not see how it was possible to get the 79th Armoured Division's divisional history published and printed in Hamburg, but this is what happened. For the officers of the 79th Armoured Division, knowing full well that the Division would be disbanded at the end of hostilities, determined that their exploits should not go unrecorded. There was one way to ensure this, and that was to publish, themselves, while in Germany, thus not giving the War Office (as it then was) the opportunity to say 'no'. How, at that time, they were able to find an intact printing works in Hamburg is something else I have never understood for the whole city was flat, but, somehow, they managed it.

Then there was the following remarkable story. I cannot vouch for it, for B Squadron did not take part in this. It is as related to me by a member of the Battalion's A Squadron.

An outing was offered to the German naval base at Kiel, and interested members of A Squadron duly piled into a 3 tonner lorry and amused themselves during the journey playing cards. The lorry was covered in, so they had no view of the surroundings.

However, glancing occasionally out of the open back of the lorry, it occurred to the party that British military traffic was not so thick as it had been and eventually that there seemed to be no traffic at all. Odd, but during the war one became used to odd situations, so no one took any particular notice.

The lorry duly pulled up with a shrieking of brakes, on the main quay at Kiel and promptly lit a petrol fire in a punctured tin can and proceeded, in traditional British Army fashion, to 'brew up' a cup of tea.

Having seen to 'first things first', the party then took some notice of their surroundings and it occurred to them that there were no British personnel around, while in the harbour the German heavy cruiser *Hipper* was blazing away from the fire on board caused by the latest RAF raid.

When some German marines with fixed bayonets began to investigate them, it eventually occurred to the bemused party that things were not as they should be. In fact, Kiel had not yet been captured. So, as unobtrusively as possible, tea-making operations were abandoned and the party re-mounted their lorry and made off with all possible speed, no worse for their adventure.

But, for B Squadron 'Corpse' the war ended appropriately with a whimper, in a manner appropriate to the deceased, in hospital.

For years previously, I had suffered from periodic stomach trouble, which of course had not been improved by Army food in general and by the liberal quantities of sand ingested while in the Palestine desert. I think the Squadron medical officer – a former vet – knew very well that I had a duodenal ulcer and, as soon as hostilities were officially over, consigned me to the small military hospital established at Lauenburg. There, they did their best to locate the ulcer, but, understandably, their X-Ray apparatus was not sufficiently sophisticated.

So, after a not unpleasant restful interlude in this hospital, I was duly packed into a Dakota aircraft and flown back to England. Not a comfortable journey, for the aircraft was just a shell, and one had to lie on the floor. For once, the sight of the green fields of England was really welcome, and particularly the verdant county of Herefordshire.

So followed a very pleasant interlude, for I was not really ill, in the civilian hospital in the City of Hereford, wearing hospital blue uniform. True they were still unable positively to identify the duodenal ulcer, but they knew very well that there was one. Meanwhile, life was made even more pleasant by picnic tea parties with one of the very temporary lady friends who have punctuated my life. I imagine the lady was attracted by a 'wounded soldier', even if he was not wounded at all but had a very prosaic ordinary ailment. It took a Birmingham teaching hospital finally to locate the ulcer, some years later.

Anyway, the 'Corpse' was appropriately pronounced as medical category C2, and thus unfit for further service. So I obtained my discharge, somewhat ahead of general demobilisation, in October 1945. Army service ended on a note of sheer horror at the demobilisation centre at York, where one was issued with a 'demob' suit, etc.

One final incident, typical of Army lack of imagination, sticks in my mind. When handing in Army uniform and kit, a paratrooper, a wearer of the famous 'Red Beret', asked the quartermaster sergeant if he could keep his beret, of which he was justifiably proud, to be told, 'NO.' He then asked if he could not buy it from the Army, to be told again very brusquely, 'NO.' Of course, it would have been just thrown away. I had great sympathy for this lad, for I, also, would have liked to have kept my, less famous, black beret, even though wearing it, not old age, had created a bald patch on top.

So, farewell to my alter ego, 'B Squadron Corpse'. The 'Corpse' little thought then that he would still be going at age 84. And I returned, like so many, to a badly interrupted career.